Intermediate Science
Through
Children's Literature

Intermediate Science Through Children's Literature

Over Land and Sea

Carol M. Butzow
John W. Butzow

Illustrations by Greg Kuhar

1994
TEACHER IDEAS PRESS
A Division of
Libraries Unlimited, Inc.
Englewood, Colorado

TEACHER IDEAS PRESS
A Division of Libraries Unlimited, Inc.
P.O. Box 6633
Englewood, CO 80155-6633
1-800-237-6124

Project Editor: Kevin W. Perizzolo
Copy Editor: Connie Hardesty
Proofreader: Eileen Bartlett
Design and Layout: Kay Minnis
Indexing: Linda Bentley

Library of Congress Cataloging-in-Publication Data

Butzow, Carol M., 1942-
    Intermediate science through children's literature : over land and sea / Carol M. Butzow and John W. Butzow.
    xxv, 193 p. 22x28 cm.
    Includes bibliographical references and index.
    ISBN 0-87287-946-1
    1. Science--Study and teaching (Elementary) 2. Environmental sciences--Study and teaching (Elementary) 3. Children's literature--Study and teaching (Elementary) I. Butzow, John W., 1939-
II. Title.
    LB1585.B84   1994
    372.3'57--dc20   94-13769
                                                              CIP

To our daughters, Kristen and Karen

Contents

Part I
Over Land

Part II
Over Sea

Preface

For the most part, science is taught in an expository mode. Students are expected to memorize facts and use skills in isolation. This experience lends itself to mental activity, but it does not necessarily provide an increase in knowledge or facilitate the ability to reason and to see relationships. While students must acquire factual knowledge, it is more important that they understand the conceptual framework that relates facts to one another and—equally important—to the world as they know it. The link between the student's knowledge and new information, or the familiar and the unfamiliar, is the point at which learning takes place.

Expository science textbooks and teaching methods do little to help students make that link because such texts and teaching methods offer little connection between the student and what is to be learned. This can be remedied by the use of texts and teaching methods that incorporate narratives, or stories.

Young people find it easier to assimilate new ideas when they are presented in stories. Stories conform to the thought processes by which students interpret information. Young people tell us what they know mainly through the use of the narrative. They speak using stories, and they understand what others say in the context of stories. They do not speak or think in the abstract terms of categories or theories but in the tangible terms of characters, settings, and events. While students do need to learn to abstract information, that skill must be developed from a foundation of knowledge. Before dealing in the abstract, students must first assimilate ideas.

Fictional literature can be used as the foundation of science instruction. Narratives present new information in the context of a story, and students find it easier to understand and assimilate ideas in this context than in the isolation and abstraction of a science textbook. Fiction presents facts and concepts in a form that encourages students to build a hypothesis, predict events, and test to determine whether their ideas are correct. In this way, the narrative first encourages assimilation of ideas and then encourages skills built upon that assimilation.

Young people need to develop powers to abstract information to comprehend or integrate the instructional concepts. The use of stories as an integral part of the intermediate science class allows students to understand, relate, and assimilate concepts. This method of instruction helps students make developmentally appropriate connections between scientific knowledge and its application.

Teachers must help students realize that science is the discovery of the world around them. To do this, science instruction must be more connected to students' experience and less dependent on formal verbal instruction. Active learning can promote individual conceptual growth, which is the ultimate goal of science instruction.

Changing Science and the Intermediate Curriculum

There is a need to change the intermediate science curriculum. This can be accomplished by building on knowledge of how children construct meaning, the developmental stages they encounter as they mature, their need for meaningful learning activities, and their reliance on narrative to find relevance. Young people do not see the natural world as scientists do.

Most science curricula ignore students' preconceived notions or concepts. Such curricula assume that students have no knowledge or that any knowledge they do have can be easily altered. This is misleading; most of the time students' views are strong and persistent, and students try to reconcile new information with the old.

Teachers must introduce scientific concepts as important, meaningful, and comprehensible entities. They must organize knowledge and link it to the students' prior knowledge. Students must understand that, although accurate scientific concepts may differ from or even conflict with students' previous ideas, the concepts can be understood. As students become goal-oriented and skilled in constructing knowledge, they become independent learners who possess an effective repertoire of comprehension strategies. Active engagement in thinking, asking, and problem solving can be achieved through experience, reading, discussion, and writing.

By reconstructing the curriculum and teaching methods for the student as an imaginative thinker, a new model of learning is constructed. Meaning is at the forefront. Lessons and units are good stories, not objectives. In this setting lessons stimulate students' imaginations and provide meaningful experiences. The curriculum is matched to the interests and abilities of students, with topics selected and sequenced according to the students' developmental levels. By expanding scientific literacy through the use of literature and other meaningful techniques, such as discovery and hands-on experiences, teachers simultaneously excite and educate students.

Using This Book

This book suggests an approach to science instruction that integrates literature as an alternative form of instruction or to enrich textbook instruction. Although literature can be used to motivate students and to provide background for the science class, as suggested by Dole and Johnson or Guerra and Payne, this is not its only function. Nor is fiction merely a means of clarifying concepts presented by other methods (Smardo). Nor are vicarious experiences from literature a substitute for direct experience and hands-on exploration. Literature, in and of itself, can be the actual factual and conceptual basis of a science lesson.

This approach uses conceptually and factually correct works of fiction. The emphasis is on earth science and life science. The physical sciences, as they relate to these topics, are fully integrated into each chapter. There is much integration across the natural sciences, the social sciences, and the arts. Content integration is a natural outcome of presenting a topic broadly. For example, a unit of study on the Arctic includes work in science, math, anthropology, geography, and the arts. This integration demonstrates the broad nature of scientific concepts and makes science more meaningful and relevant.

In the activities outlined in this book, students should be allowed to do the majority of the work, with the teacher acting as the facilitator. For this reason instructions in the book are written to the students, not to the teacher. Occasional notes to the teacher are included when certain parts of activities must be performed by the teacher. In class discussions teachers should not rely on formal questions but encourage students to develop and express their thoughts and feelings.

Many of the activities in this book require cooperation among faculty. The classroom teacher, specialty area teachers, and the library media specialist form a team with each specialist contributing to specific activities. Where there are teachers for each subject area, greater cooperation is required. All teachers must agree on the novel to be read; that novel provides the focus of instruction for all areas of study. This requires cooperation in selecting the novel, scheduling the unit, and coordinating activities. Science content is covered by the science teacher, geographical setting and implication by the social studies teacher and so on. Language arts teachers do reading or writing projects based on the book and assist students in writing science journals or reports for other classes. Math problems transcend topic areas by covering data collection and analysis, maps, and charts.

A wide variety of activities are provided for each novel, including hands-on activities, field trips, craft projects, library research, and collateral reading and writing. The activities are a series of alternatives upon which the teacher can build instructional sequences. The activities can be done in any order, or they can stand alone. Teachers may feel free to choose only those activities that suit their classroom environment, student abilities, and schedule.

While the activities in this book can stand alone, they also can be modified to accompany a specific lesson in a science text. For example, the activities that emphasize rock structure can be used in conjunction with a science text on geology.

The novels selected for this book are the works of authors who relate scientific ideas to everyday life. Authors like Gary Paulsen and Jean Craighead George relate the experiences of children in unusual environments and situations in such a way that the unusual seems everyday to the reader.

Because of the age level and nature of the curriculum at this level, the lessons and novels used in this book are primarily concerned with the environment, specifically the land and the sea. Following an introduction to teaching methods and strategies, the book is divided into two parts. The first part deals with the land—prairies, tornadoes, the north woods, fossils, and so forth—and the second part deals with the sea—coral reefs, tropical lagoons, freshwater lakes, and wetlands.

References

Dole, Janice A., and Virginia R. Johnson. "Beyond the Textbook: Science Literature for Young People." *Journal of Reading* 24 (1981): 579–82.

Guerra, Cathy, and Delores B. Payne. "Using Popular Books and Magazines to Interest Students in General Science." *Journal of Reading* 24 (1981): 583–85.

Smardo, Frances A. "Using Children's Literature to Clarify Science Concepts in Early Childhood Programs." *Reading Teacher* 36 (1982): 267–73.

Acknowledgments

To the Northern New England Marine Education Project, University of Maine, for permission to adapt the illustrations related to ocean life.

To Mr. Kim Fry, for the loan of newspapers pertaining to the tornadoes that hit Grand Island, Nebraska.

To Dr. Robert P. Sechrist, for the map of Colorado.

To the Ontario Ministry of Tourism, for the map of Lake Windigo.

To Mr. Steve Webster, for "Hark! I Phelt a Knudge."

To the members of the Teacher Enhancement Institute, Latrobe, PA 1992 and 1993, who helped field test several of these units.

To the many teachers who attended our workshops and conferences, for accepting and implementing our ideas, and encouraging us to write a follow-up to *Science Through Children's Literature*.

To our parents who always support and encourage our ideas and work.

Introduction

A recent definition gives broad meaning to the concept of science. Noted science educator Robert Yager describes science as "anything that promotes explanation, encourages the creation of explanations, or calls for verification and validation" (Yager et al.). Science should not be seen as a list of concepts or memorized vocabulary, facts, and procedures. Instead, science should emphasize learning how to learn through the use of problem solving, original thinking, discovery, inquiry, and hands-on activities.

Problem solving and discovery take place when learners take the initiative, when they use their abilities to discover concepts or principles. In this case students are active, not passive, learners. As active learners they discover knowledge and then integrate it.

When lessons are concrete, students achieve higher levels of success. Hands-on activities are important to both cognitive achievement and science achievement. Concrete, hands-on activities allow students to become involved in learning and to use higher forms of questions such as analysis, synthesis, and evaluation.

As with other subject areas, learning science involves interaction between new and existing concepts. Learners actively build knowledge by using existing knowledge to interpret new information in ways that make sense to them. Many young people come to science class with preconceived ideas and interpretations about the material to be studied. Although they have had no formal instruction about the topic, they have learned about it through personal experience or the media. However, many of the students' ideas and interpretations are scientifically incorrect or inadequate. The strength of these misconceptions can make it difficult for learners to restructure their background knowledge to accommodate new information. If students cannot accommodate new material, they become passive learners. Material will not be integrated into their experience and will be soon forgotten.

Learning occurs when the learner consciously links new knowledge to existing concepts. This assimilation is effective only when the new knowledge is inherently meaningful or useful. It is not rote learning but problem solving and hands-on activities that facilitate the retention of new concepts. Stories that contain cause and effect relationships that relate to readers' prior knowledge provide the basis of comprehension.

One of the most common and concrete means of imparting knowledge is narrative, or story. Narrative is formed by the causal linkage of events. By providing context, narrative gives meaning to events and makes connections among them. Stories provide clear beginnings and endings and a rhythm of expectation and satisfaction that young people need.

Literature encourages readers to go beyond the superficial, low-level comprehension encouraged by abstract texts to engage in higher-order thinking skills, such as inference, comparison, and drawing conclusions.

Children are not alone in using stories to communicate or understand. All humans tend to communicate by telling stories. Our eagerness to listen to and tell stories takes many forms and serves many functions. We frequently transform our experiences, and what we read or hear, into stories. We share and compare our experiences. Narrative helps us to interpret relationships, motives, feelings, and consequences.

Literature for young people is written by authors who know young people and who extend reality by presenting familiar things in new light. Skillful use of language heightens excitement and sharpens readers' thinking skills by encouraging the use of interpretation and comprehension. For example, encouraging students to predict while reading strengthens deductive processes.

Science Instruction

Typically, science is taught using traditional textbooks and worksheets. Subject matter is broken into isolated bits bearing little meaning and relevance to the students' lives (McCutcheon and Burton). Concept and practical application of ideas are often omitted or touched upon so briefly that students develop a misconception about science (Eaton, Anderson, and Smith). Teachers may regard textbooks as so many pages to cover, while their pupils tally how many tasks they must complete. Watching and performing experiments will not satisfy the needs of students unless they have learned the language and thinking intrinsic to science (Guerra and Payne). Even hands-on activities will not produce comprehension if misconceptions are not addressed and new concepts explained and made relevant (Eaton, Anderson, and Smith).

Narrative is rarely used in the typical science classroom. Eighty-five percent of classrooms are dominated by textbooks that present factual information; they do not provide a means of learning the skills involved in critical thinking and problem solving. These textbooks are product-oriented rather than process-oriented. They stress the correct answer, not how to arrive at the answer. But, just as there are many ways to solve a problem, there are many ways to reach a conclusion. Science textbooks that present only abstract facts are not really addressed to learners; they are addressed to some abstract concept of student.

The tools of scientific inquiry—observation, communication, classification, measurement, prediction, and inference—lend themselves perfectly to the process of learning. Emphasizing these skills in the classroom reflects the objectives of science and helps students to discover answers. Likewise, basic reading strategies—observation, comparison and contrast, detection of cause and effect, conclusion, sequence, judgment and analogy, and evaluation—are relevant to science. Both science and reading instruction equip learners to reason, to link various areas of knowledge, and to identify relationships.

Narrative piques students' interests and heightens their enthusiasm and responsiveness by expanding their relationship to the world. Narratives allow students to see facts in ways not generally used in the science classroom. Literature teaches problem solving, observation skills, creative writing, and vocabulary. Concepts learned in reading fiction, biography, newspapers, and other narrative materials provide the impetus for scientific research and experimentation.

Science instruction should be holistic and conceptual, with activities that emphasize problem solving and application. Stories have a place in the science curriculum as a source of conceptual knowledge and experiential background.

Holistic Science

To understand the use of literature in science instruction it is necessary to understand the whole language or holistic philosophy of teaching. The holistic approach is based on a constructivist view of learning, that is, that learners actively build their own knowledge by interpreting new information in light of what they already know. The holistic philosophy is put into practice when students are allowed to develop explanations as they solve problems and to look for ways that science affects their lives. For example, students learning about weather would observe cloud formations and the weather, drawing conclusions about cause and effect relationships. Then students apply what they have learned by predicting the weather. The holistic approach employs many sources of authentic materials as readings, springboards for discussion, and bases for activities, experimentation, and inquiry.

Whole language means that students read for information, ideas, insights, and entertainment, all at once. In this way students learn that print makes sense and language can be learned naturally through reading, writing, listening, and speaking. Skills are not separated into isolated hierarchies, nor are subject areas compartmentalized.

Knowledge and learning reach across lines that divide disciplines to create a total learning experience. Literature provides a bridge between content and context. The teacher must balance the content and context. Activities that help teachers achieve this balance follow; some of the suggestions are directed at teachers and some are directed at students.

Reading Activities

Read to students every day.

Schedule sustained silent reading for students on a regular basis.

Read additional books by the author who wrote the text being studied.

Read narrative and expository books on the same topic.

Read a biography of the author.

Read each other's writing.

Arrange for students to read to younger children.

Have a "real world" reading corner with magazines, telephone books, catalogs, TV guides, reference books, newspapers, etc.

Set up a classroom library of recreational reading books that represent all literary genres. Include books written by students, if possible.

Read and follow recipes.

Practice telling a story, then tape it.

Writing Activities

Schedule sustained silent writing time, during which students write about topics they select or about specified topics, for example, "If I had my choice, I would like to be ... " or "My favorite character was ... ."

Write stories, including language experience stories.

Keep journals.

Keep reading logs.

Write poems and descriptions.

Draw and label maps, charts, and diagrams.

Write letters to each other, to authors, to characters in books, and to others.

Sequence events of a story using words or pictures.

Edit each other's writing.

Rewrite or edit using a word processor.

Predict the ending of the story and write it.

Rewrite the story's ending or create a sequel to the story.

Create multiple endings for a story and see which one is most popular.

Publish a class newspaper.

Adapt stories to radio dramas, plays, or television programs.

Write book reviews.

Summarize the story for a book jacket or bulletin board display.

Think of interview questions to ask a guest who will visit the class.

Rewrite the major action or events of the story from the viewpoint of another character.

Keep personal dictionaries of key words from stories or words of special interest.

Make up or complete word searches, crossword puzzles, word games, or acrostics that are related to the lesson.

Write directions and have someone follow them.

Keep a card file of all books read by students and the teacher on each major topic; categorize the books as fiction and nonfiction.

Make a question box to hold inquiries about the topic being studied. Once a week open the box and answer the questions.

Write scientific experiments and results.

Make time lines using long sheets of shelf paper or heavy twine knotted every few inches to represent a certain number of years.

Have a letterwriting corner and a post office.

Write directions for plant care, animal feeding, etc. Post the instructions.

Post explanations or rules for fire drills, going to the library, special class changes, etc.

Create bulletin boards, attendance sheets, job charts, and signup rosters for students to maintain.

Provide a message board for communicating with the teacher and among students.

Set up a weather station, including devices to measure temperature, wind speed, and wind direction. Study daily weather maps in a newspaper. Keep materials on hand to measure and record local sky and wind conditions and precipitation.

Use calendars to keep track of classroom events, or use annotated calendars indicating famous events, birthdays, honorary weeks, etc.

Discussion Topics

Retell a story as a comprehension check.

Use direct instruction and modeling to gain insight into text components, such as plot, setting, character, or theme, or skills, such as inference, cause and effect, prediction, sequence, comparison, and drawing conclusions.

Hold panel discussions and debates.

Conduct interviews and discussions with outside speakers, each other, or students role playing characters from the book.

Practice and give oral book reviews (*not* book reports).

Play "Who Said That?" to identify important lines from the book or "This Is Your Life" to review the accomplishments of the characters.

Think of new titles for a book and discuss whether they are meaningful.

What else do you want to know about the topic? How can you find out? Check out your ideas.

Learn about the historical and geographical setting of the story if it is integral to the concepts of the story.

Discuss the author's purpose in writing the book.

Art

Make cartoons of the action in the story and sequence them.

Draw pictures depicting characters or events in the story.

Design book jackets.

Make advertisements or bulletin board displays about the book or its scientific concepts.

Write a commercial to encourage people to buy or read the book.

Build dioramas or paint murals suggested by the setting of the book.

Design a coat of arms for a major character using symbols to show the accomplishments of his or her life.

Label exhibits and collections of objects pertaining to the book.

Sketch or make costumes like those the characters wore (use dolls or people as models).

Show photos or slides to provide background to the book.

Assemble a collage of pictures showing concepts or events in the story.

Invent a competitive board game about the story; include questions on vocabulary, events, characters, sequences, etc.

Bring in magazine and newspaper articles that are relevant to the story.

Start a fan club for your favorite author or character; include membership cards, buttons, newsletters, etc.

Drama and Media

Present choral readings by large groups, groups in the class, or soloists.

Tape dramatizations in the style of the old radio shows.

Produce videotapes in which the story is acted out.

Pantomime events or concepts of the story.

Improvise or role play part of the story, an alternate ending, a scientific happening, etc.

Compare the book to a record, filmstrip, or video of the same story.

Serialize the book in some dramatic form and present it over several days.

Pretend to be a movie director and cast the characters in the book for television or a film.

Practice, then give dramatic readings.

Select appropriate music to go with a reading or dramatization.

Bridging the Gap Between Science and Literature

In the traditional, factual approach to teaching science, experimentation was an end in itself. Knowledge was regarded as background information needed for future science studies or in adulthood. Explanations were given before students experimented or read, with the result that discovery, learning, critical thinking, and problem solving were minimized. Integration of curriculum, use of narrative forms, and extended writing were nowhere to be found. However, as stated before, students learn not in the abstract but in the concrete. Literature provides a bridge between the abstract and the concrete.

Many forms of literature can help young people learn about science, including picture books, novels, poetry, traditional stories, anecdotes, biographies, books about discoveries and inventions, newspapers, magazines, popular science books, journals, diaries, and letters. All of human history is a story, and science can be seen as a means of telling that story. Paleontologists are storytellers, for geology is the story of the earth; chemical reactions are stories in the form of equations. To what extent do scientists understand processes and principles except by mastering a set of stories? Have not the important scientific discoveries resulted from innovative, plausible stories about the world?

Contemporary science writers use storytelling forms to present material. The works of writers like Carl Sagan and Isaac Asimov marry story and exposition. By using a narrative structure that makes science both interesting and significant, these writers have made the complex and detailed workings of science comprehensible to the general public.

Integrating Subjects into Science Education

Many novels are grounded in fact and provide unique perspectives on history, languages, the arts, and technical subjects. It follows naturally that, as the use of literature in the science curriculum expands, other curricular areas will come into play. The relationship is complementary: Literature provides enrichment for science, and science and other curricular areas provide information and context for understanding literature. By its very nature, literature as a tool for teaching science assumes integration of subjects. This integration expands the nature of learning, for literature develops cognitive values and discussions about literature develop the affective domain.

Writing in Science

Students must write in the science class. Writing is a means of achieving understanding and of making connections between what students are learning and what they already know. In this style of teaching, writing is not filling in factual answers, defining vocabulary words, or writing structured lab reports. Rather, writing in the science class takes the form of daily learning logs, biographical sketches, research reports, summaries, anecdotal observations, and self-evaluations. Students may write explanations of how and why events occur, predictions, observations, and reactions to readings.

Textbooks give the impression that knowledge is a given and cannot be disputed or altered. In fact, however, facts and concepts become significant only when they are related to other facts and when connections are made among them. These connections are best illustrated by the use of literature and the integration of traditional curricula. As we have seen, literature provides more than facts. It stresses problem solving and critical thinking and fosters the use of precise descriptive language. Literature covers the span of human experience, offering meaning and information not found in textbooks.

References

References Cited

Eaton, Janet, Charles Anderson, and Edward Smith. *Students' Misconceptions Interfere with Learning: Case Studies of Fifth Grade Students.* Lansing: Michigan State University, Institute for Research on Teaching, 1983.

Guerra, Cathy, and Delores B. Payne. "Using Popular Books and Magazines to Interest Students in General Science." *Journal of Reading* 24 (1981): 583–85.

McCutcheon, Gail, and Frederick Burton. *A Qualitative Study of Children's Responses to Textbook Centered Classrooms* (Research/technical 143). Columbus: Ohio State University, 1981.

Yager, Robert, John McLure, and Jeffrey Weld. "Applying Science across the Curriculum" *Educational Leadership.* Volume 50 (May 1993): 79.

Reading, Whole Language, and Science

Butzow, Carol M. *A Comparison of a Storyline Based Method of Instruction and a Textbook Method of Instruction on the Acquisition of Science Concepts in the Elementary School.* Ann Arbor, Mich.: University Microfilms, May 1992. Publication number 9209536 Volume issue 511.

Driver, Rosalind, Edith Guesne, and Andree Tiberghien, eds. *Children's Ideas in Science.* Milton Keynes, England: Open University Press, 1985.

Goodman, Kenneth. *What's Whole in Whole Language?* Portsmouth, N.H.: Heinemann Educational Books, 1986.

Hansen, Jane, Thomas Newkirk, and Donald Graves, eds. *Breaking Ground.* Portsmouth, N.H.: Heinemann Educational Books, 1985.

Holdaway, Don. *The Foundations of Literacy.* Portsmouth, N.H.: Heinemann Educational Books, 1979.

Huck, Charlotte, and Doris Kuhn. *Children's Literature in the Elementary School.* 4th ed. New York: Holt, Rinehart & Winston, 1987.

Martin, Kathleen, and E. Miller. "Storytelling and Science." *Language Arts* 65 (1988): 255–59.

National Research Council. *Fulfilling the Promise: Biology Education in the Nation's Schools.* Washington, D.C.: National Academy Press, 1990.

Newman, Judith M., ed. *Whole Language Theory in Use.* Portsmouth, N.H.: Heinemann Educational Books, 1985.

Osborne, Roger, and Peter Freyberg. *Learning in Science.* Portsmouth, N.H.: Heinemann Educational Books, 1988.

Rosen, Harold. "The Importance of Story." *Language Arts* 63 (1986): 226–37.

Smith, Frank. *Reading without Nonsense.* 2d ed. New York: Columbia University, Teachers College, 1985.

Wells, Gordon. *The Meaning Makers: Children Learning Language and Using Language to Learn.* Portsmouth, N.H.: Heinemann Educational Books, 1986.

Science Activity Books

Abruscato, Joseph, and Jack Hassard. *The Earth People Activity Book: People, Places, Pleasures and Other Delights.* Glenview, Ill.: Scott, Foresman, 1978.

_____. *The Whole Cosmos Catalog of Science Activities.* Glenview, Ill.: Scott, Foresman, 1978.

Bonnet, Robert, and G. Daniel Keen. *Earth Science: 49 Science Fair Projects.* Blue Ridge Summit, Pa.: TAB Books, 1990.

_____. *Environmental Science: 49 Science Fair Projects.* Blue Ridge Summit, Pa.: TAB Books, 1990.

_____. *Space and Astronomy: 49 Science Fair Projects.* Blue Ridge Summit, Pa.: TAB Books, 1992.

Butzow, Carol M., and John W. Butzow. *Science through Children's Literature.* Englewood, Colo.: Libraries Unlimited, Teacher Ideas Press, 1989.

Comstock, Anna B. *Handbook of Nature Study.* Ithaca, N.Y.: Cornell University Press, 1986.

Cornell, Joseph B. *Sharing Nature with Children.* Nevada City, Calif.: Dawn Publications, 1979.

DeBruin, Jerry. *Creative, Hands-on Science Experiences.* Carthage, Ill.: Good Apple, 1986.

Gardner, Martin. *Entertaining Science Experiments with Everyday Objects.* New York: Dover Publications, 1981.

Gates, Julie M. *Consider the Earth: Environmental Activities for Grades 4–8.* Englewood, Colo.: Libraries Unlimited, Teacher Ideas Press, 1989.

Gems Project Staff. *Once Upon a Gems Guide: Connecting Young People's Literature to Great Explorations in Math and Science.* Berkeley, Calif.: Lawrence Hall of Science, 1993.

Hanauer, Ethel. *Biology Experiments for Children.* New York: Dover Publications, 1968.

Kohl, MaryAnn, and Cindy Gainer. *Good Earth Art.* Mt. Rainier, Md.: Gryphon House, 1991.

Lowery, Lawrence, and Carol Verbeeck. *Explorations in Earth Science.* Belmont, Calif.: David S. Lake, 1987.

_____. *Explorations in Life Science.* Belmont, Calif.: David S. Lake, 1987.

_____. *Explorations in Physical Science.* Belmont, Calif.: David S. Lake, 1987.

Mullin, Virginia L. *Chemistry Experiments for Children*. New York: Dover Publications, 1968.

Ontario Science Centre. *Foodworks*. Toronto: Kids Can Press, 1986.

Ontario Science Centre. *Sportsworks*. Toronto: Kids Can Press, 1989.

Outdoor Biology Instructional Strategies (OBIS). Nashua, N.H.: Delta Education, 1982.

Pilger, Mary Anne. *Science Experiments Index for Young People*. Englewood, Colo.: Libraries Unlimited, 1988. (Available in print version and on computer disk.).

Reuben, Gabriel. *Electricity Experiments for Children*. New York: Dover Publications, 1968.

Savan, Beth. *Earthcycles and Ecosystems*. Toronto: Kids Can Press, 1991.

Stenmark, Jean Kerr, Virginia Thompson, and Ruth Cossey. *Family Math*. Berkeley, Calif.: Lawrence Hall of Science, 1986.

VanCleave, Janice. *Astronomy for Every Kid*. New York: John Wiley, 1991.

Vivian, Charles. *Science Experiments and Amusements for Children*. New York: Dover Publications, 1967.

Professional Journals and Magazines for Young People

Booklist. American Library Association, Chicago, Ill. Published semimonthly.

Hornbook. Horn Book, Boston, Mass. Published six times a year.

Language Arts. National Council of Teachers of English, Urbana, Ill. Published seven times a year.

National Geographic World. National Geographic Society, Washington, D.C. Published monthly.

Ranger Rick. National Wildlife Foundation, Vienna, Va. Published monthly.

The Reading Teacher. International Reading Association, Newark, Del. Published nine times a year.

School Library Journal. R. R. Bowker, New York. Published ten times a year.

School Science and Mathematics. School Science and Mathematics Association, Bowling Green, Ohio. Published eight times a year.

Science and Children. National Science Teachers Association, Washington, D.C. Published eight times a year.

Science Scope. National Science Teachers Association, Washington, D.C. Published eight times a year.

Part I
Over Land

Chapter 1

The American Prairie

Sarah, Plain and Tall

Patricia MacLachlan
New York: Harper & Row, 1985

Summary

Sarah, Plain and Tall is the story of a woman who lives in two very different environments—her original home on the coast of Maine and her new home on the American prairie. Having answered a widower's letter for a bride to help raise two young children, Sarah finds the vast openness of the prairie more isolating than her home in Maine. Eventually, as her new family accepts her and she learns to love her husband, Jacob, Sarah accepts the Midwest as her home.

Earth Concepts

Agriculture, prairie ecosystem, vegetation, soil, climate, storms and weather, marine versus land ecosystems, intertidal zone (ocean)

Environmental Concepts

Relationship of shelter and weather, protection from storms, positive and negative effects of wind, determination of vegetation by climate

General Concepts

Frontier life in the late 1800s and early 1900s, women's roles, death and adjustment, stepfamily relationships, transportation and distance, moving and homesickness, habitat

Activities

1. After you read *Sarah, Plain and Tall,* work with your classmates to list the parts of the farm described in the book, for example, the house, barn, or pond. Write each word on a separate card. Create a map of the farm on a large sheet of paper or bulletin board. Place the cards that name the parts of the farm in their relative positions according to the description of the farm in *Sarah, Plain and Tall,* and then draw in fields and roads.

   Close your eyes and visualize the farm. To help you visualize, your teacher will talk you through a tour of the farm. As you imagine yourself seeing the things your teacher describes, look for people, animals, plants, buildings, and other things mentioned in *Sarah, Plain and Tall.*

2. This book takes place on the American prairie. The prairie biome (or type of ecosystem) is a vast, relatively treeless area. A thick layer of sod covers very rich soil. To investigate the layers of earth in your area, make a soil profile.

   a. Have a teacher or other adult dig a hole about 24 inches deep in an area where this activity is permissable. This is deep enough to reveal major differences in most soils.

   b. Collect about a cup of each type of soil or rock found from the top to the bottom of the hole. Also collect a sample of the sod covering. Notice the different plant and animal forms present in the sod.

   c. Draw a diagram or photograph a cross section of the soil layers showing their depth and texture and how they join. See figure 1.1 below. Children should view the hole in small groups under teacher supervision. Be sure the hole is filled in before returning to the classroom.

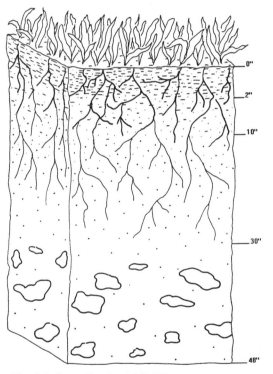

Fig. 1.1. Cross Section of Soil Layers.

   d. In the classroom make a poster-size version of the soil profile. Be sure to include the sod layer. Glue soil and rock samples to the poster.

3. Compare the water-retaining properties of soil and sod. Place two buckets side by side. In one bucket place a shovelful of soil; in the second bucket place a shovelful of sod. Pour two liters of water over each sample. Weigh each bucket. Leave them uncovered for a week and weigh them again. Observe the differences in weight and the appearance of the soil and sod. What does this tell you about sod's ability to retain moisture?

4. Gather samples of various types of soil from the area in which you live. If you can, ask friends who live elsewhere to send you about 2 cups of soil.

   a. Using a hand lens compare the soils for color, organic material, and texture. Also compare their odor and how they feel.

b. Measure half a cup of each of several types of soil. Mix the samples in a large glass jar with a tight-fitting lid. Cover the mixture with water, put on the lid, and shake the jar vigorously. Let the soil settle for several days. What do you see? If possible, leave the jar in place until the end of the school year and observe the changes in the soil.

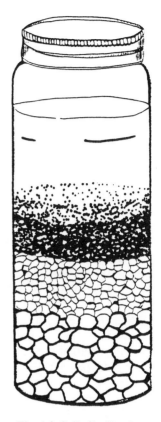

c. Cut the top 6 inches off a 2-liter bottle. Turn the top piece of the bottle upside down and set it in the bottom piece. This makes a funnel. Make a funnel for each soil sample. Put a coffee filter in each funnel. Place a different type of growing medium in each funnel. Use sand, potting soil, peat moss, crushed stone, and three or four locally obtained soil samples. Saturate each sample with water. After three or four days, compare the moisture content of each sample. Compare again after a week. What can you deduce about the best soil for raising crops?

Fig. 1.2. Soils Settling in a Container.

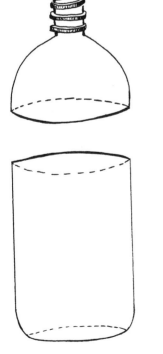

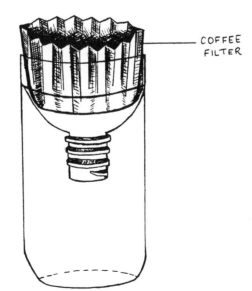

COFFEE FILTER

Fig. 1.3. Soil Activity Equipment.

5. For information, activities, and overhead transparencies on soil and soil conservation, write to the U.S. Department of Agriculture Soil Conservation Service. U.S.D.A.; P.O. Box 2890, Washington, DC 20013-2890.

6. To learn about the status of the prairie today, read "The Tallgrass Prairie: Can It Be Saved?" by Dennis Farney in *National Geographic* (volume 157, number 1, January 1985) or "Roots of the Sky" by Douglas Chadwick in *National Geographic* (volume 184, number 4, October 1993).

7. Many farmers depend on fertilizers to increase the yield of their crops. To see how commercial or organic fertilizers affect the growth of plants, apply various kinds of fertilizer to the plants in your classroom. For best results, follow the directions carefully.

8. Animals that inhabit the prairie include killdeer, meadowlarks, sandpipers, short-eared owls, marsh hawks, turkey buzzards, wild turkeys, golden eagles, rattlesnakes, prairie dogs, ground squirrels, cottontail rabbits, weasels, coyotes, bobcats, white-tailed deer, pronghorn, elk, and bison. Why do these animals live in the same area? Make a predator–prey chart for these animals and preserve it as a bulletin board.

9. Hail can ruin an entire crop in minutes. Look in a weather or science book to see how hail is formed. What weather conditions precede and follow a hailstorm? Ask your parents or grandparents if they remember any hailstorms. See if the library media center has newspaper reports of hailstorms.

10. High winds can devastate a field of grain but can produce power when harnessed by a windmill. You can build a windmill. Many large erector sets, plastic building blocks, or wooden construction sets include parts to make a windmill that can be hooked up to a motor. Make a windmill, hook the motor to a light bulb, and turn the blades of the windmill with a small fan or hair dryer.

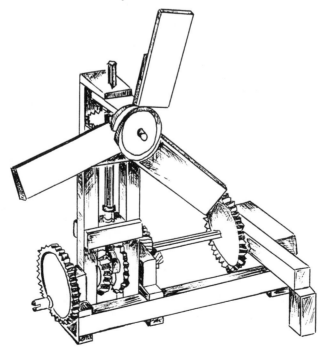

Fig. 1.4. Working Model of a Windmill.

11. At the turn of the century, farms on the prairie depended on wind power. Look in an almanac to find out which areas of the United States have the highest average wind speed. Locate each area on a map of the United States. Which areas are in the Great Plains? Those are the areas in which windmills would be of most use to farmers.

12. For more activities concerning windmills, see chapter 2.

13. Sarah's farm is in a region often hit by tornadoes. See chapter 3 for activities concerning violent storms.

14. In the library media center, look for world maps that indicate cropland or land under cultivation. Which countries devote the most land area to producing food? In the United States, which states devote the most land area to food production? Compare cropland maps to topographic maps. Why is the central portion of the United States called the Great Plains? Why do grain and livestock tend to come from the same area? Are most of the major croplands of the world located on plains?

15. The Great Plains is known as the breadbasket of the nation because of the many grains grown there. Obtain samples of various whole grains—for example, popcorn, corn, wheat kernels, wild rice, oats, or barley—from grocery, feed or seed, or health food stores.

    a. Soak the grains overnight and cut them in half. This can be done by the teacher using a small, sharp knife.

    b. With a hand lens observe the parts of the seed.

    c. Drop a tiny amount of iodine on the seed. Starch will turn blue. Starch is a carbohydrate, which supplies energy to both plants and animals, including people.

    d. Sketch the grains, whole and cut in half, in your science journal. Compare the grains.

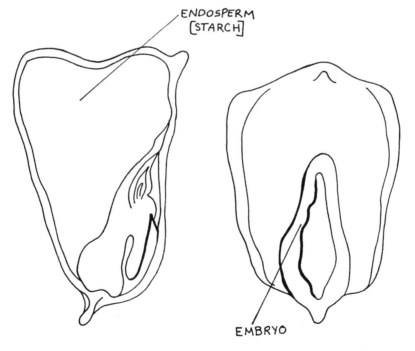

Fig. 1.5. Structure of the Corn Kernel.

16. Take a vote on which breakfast cereal is the favorite among all your classmates. Register your vote by bringing in an empty box of your favorite cereal. Make a bar graph to show which cereals are the most popular. Read the side panels of some cereal boxes to learn what kinds of grains the cereals contain, the size of each serving, and the calories per serving. Pick three or four popular cereals that have equal serving sizes and compare the following:

   protein

   sugars (be specific)

   fat

   cholesterol

   vitamins (be specific)

   potassium

   iron

   magnesium

17. How do the cereals compare as to grams of fat per serving? Do the manufacturers give nutritional breakdowns for cereal eaten with skim milk, whole milk, or 2-percent milk? If one gram of fat equals nine calories, and the cereal is eaten without milk, how many calories per serving come from fat?

18. Most cereal boxes list nutritional information for a one-ounce serving, or about half a cup. Measure out a half cup of cereal. Next measure out how much cereal you usually eat. Do you eat more than a half cup? How much more? Use the nutritional information on the side of the cereal box to calculate how many calories you consume when you eat cereal.

19. Have a taste test to see if you can identify various popular cereals by taste alone.

20. Make a TV advertisement promoting your favorite cereal.

21. Trees are not native to the vast American prairie. Settlers planted them for shade, recreation, and erosion control. Decide where your school yard could use a tree and plant one. Consult a book from your library media center to determine what kind of tree will grow best in your school's environment.

22. Sarah's farm had a windbreak of Russian olive trees. Windbreaks can be natural or man-made. On a windy day go to the school yard to find windbreaks. When it is cold or windy, where do students go during recess? Where do the teachers stand? What other kinds of windbreaks might you find elsewhere (for example, a snow fence in a field)?

23. Many wildflowers are mentioned in the book. Look them up in a wildflower guide. What climatic zones produce the wildflowers mentioned in *Sarah, Plain and Tall?* What other growing conditions are needed for these plants? Find out whether any of the wildflowers in your area are protected by law or whether any are endangered.

Fig. 1.6. Wildflowers.

24. Quilts were essential during long, cold winters on the prairie. On several sheets of $8\frac{1}{2}$-by-11-inch paper, sketch some wildflowers. Tape the sheets together to resemble a large quilt. Hang the quilt on the wall.

25. Sarah gathered wildflowers to share their beauty. If it is legal, gather wildflowers from public places or ask permission to gather them from private gardens. Decorate your classroom with fresh flowers or use them in art projects. Pressing or drying flowers preserves their beauty. To press flowers, lay them carefully between layers of newsprint and set several heavy books on top of the stack, or use a plant press. Pressed flowers can be used to decorate stationery, bookmarks, and mobiles. To dry flowers, hang bouquets upside down in a dry area. Place dried bouquets in bottles or vases.

26. Caleb made up a rhyme about a woolly ragwort. Can you write a verse or limerick about another weed or wildflower? Write each verse or limerick on a separate sheet of paper and illustrate them for a bulletin board display.

27. Sarah loved seashells because they reminded her of Maine. Make a classroom collection of shells students have collected or bought. Your teacher and other teachers may contribute to the collection. Classify the shells by shape. Use reference books to identify the type of animal that inhabited each type of shell, such as gastropods (snails) and bivalves (clams). Two common reference books for seashells are *Seashells of the World* (Golden Press) and Kenneth Gosner's *A Field Guide to the Atlantic Seashore* (Houghton Mifflin).

Fig. 1.7. Marine Shells.

28. Use a series of drawings to compare the two regions in which Sarah lived.

    a. Draw pictures of the farm, just as Sarah did for William. You may include Jacob, Anna, and Caleb in these pictures. Write a letter to accompany the pictures. In the letter describe the land, plants, crops, rocks, and sky to help William visualize the farm and prairie.

    b. Using the three colors that Sarah had—blue, gray, and green—draw pictures of the sea. Experiment with drawing waves as well as still water. Ask the art teacher for hints to help you make your drawing more realistic and three-dimensional.

29. Sarah missed her native Maine. Ask the library media specialist to help you locate pictures of Maine in books of paintings by Winslow Homer or Andrew Wyeth, in geography books, in books about lighthouses, or in curriculum files. Calendars often picture the Portland Head Light, which was commissioned by George Washington and is still in operation.

30. Compared to our lives today, Sarah lived a very isolated existence, both in Maine and on the prairie. Give examples from the story that support this claim. Do you think Sarah was more isolated in Maine or on the prairie. Why?

31. Prairie farmers grow large crops of grains, such as wheat and corn. In the classroom grind dried corn to flour using a mortar and pestle, or pound it to flour with a small hammer. To pound the corn into flour, place the grains in a plastic bag. Seal the bag and place it inside another plastic bag. Seal that bag and repeat with one more bag. Place the package on a wooden board and pound the corn gently with a small hammer or mallet. Use the corn flour to make muffins. Add blueberries to include a crop native to Maine.

32. Bread can be made from almost any grain, and it comes in various shapes and sizes. Visit a bakery to find out how many kinds of bread are made there. Taste various kinds of bread, including pumpernickel, pita, matzo, tortilla, and bagel. Try baking bread.

33. Pasta is made from wheat. Use several varieties of pasta to make a collage or to layer in a glass jar. Ask the manager of a local Italian grocery or restaurant to give you small amounts of various kinds of pasta to compare.

34. Herb gardens were found in the dooryards of many farmhouses. Unscramble the following words to learn what might have grown there. (Answers can be found on page 183.)

    asibl

    wldidele

    gase

    myhet

    mjmorraa

    mrsaoeyr

    itmn

    tongrraa

    oegroan

    labefay (2 words)

35. *Sarah, Plain and Tall* is set around the turn of the century, when writing was the major form of communication among people who lived far from one another. Characters in this book expressed their feelings in letters to their loved ones, for example, Sarah wrote to William to describe her new home and homesickness, and Papa wrote to ask Sarah to come. Think of times when other characters in the book might have written letters and to whom they might have written. [Note to teachers: This activity could serve as the beginning of a unit on writing letters.]

36. Many books and movies are continued in a sequel. Sometimes, events that led to the original story are later told in what is called a prequel. *Sarah, Plain and Tall* could be extended by a prequel or a sequel. Write a sequel or prequel to *Sarah, Plain and Tall*. Be sure your characterization is consistent with the original.

37. Jacob wrote an advertisement for a wife and mother. What do you think the advertisement would have said if Anna and Caleb had written it? Write the advertisement as Anna and Caleb might have written it. Remember, the cost of placing an advertisement is based on the word count. Set a limit on the number of words to be used, and write advertisements for purposes consistent with the story, for example, selling land, buying horses, or promoting a blacksmith's work.

B and B

Dress fabrics at 25¢ a yard
New Austrian suitings – narrow stripes, handsome colors.
$1.00 a yard

☛Mail orders
Catalog & Fashion Journal
Write for copy

BOGGS & BUHL
118–121 FEDERAL ST.
ALLEGHENY.   PENN'A

Orphan's Court Sale!
Estate of James Kerr, deceased

**Friday, October 30, 1891
At 2 o'clock P.M.**

Seventy-seven Acres
strict measure

**A Two-Story Frame House
Barn and other outbuildings**

TERMS
One-third cash, one third in one year and the balance in two years with interest to be secured by lien on premises

By James McGregor, clerk

BAUGH'S OLD STAND-BYS

INCLUDING

BONE AND POTASH COMPOUND

FOR SALE BY

**Peter Holsopple
Saint Joseph**

Every crop need and any substantial raw bone manure required for soil improvement can be supplied by Baugh and Sons Company.
Original Manufacturers of Raw Bone Phosphate

W. S. Daugherty

All kinds of rough and worked lumber

FLOORING, SIDING, CEILING

ALMOST ANYTHING THAT CAN BE MADE IN A PLANING MILL WILL BE FURNISHED AT REASONABLE RATES AND ON SHORT NOTICE

Market Prices Paid for all Kind of Good Lumber

Fig. 1.8. Advertisements for 1891 Products.

38. Going into town was a long, involved process. Compare Sarah's journey to buy the colored pencils to a trip you would make downtown or to a mall. Compare modes of transportation, clothing, food, and stores.

39. Sarah and other women of her time did not lead the kinds of lives that women do today. What are the similarities and differences? Why did Papa react as he did when Sarah came to help repair the roof? How else do you know Sarah was more liberated than many women of her time?

40. Papa sang a song in Middle English. Compare the words to modern English. See the list following the poem to learn the meaning of some of the Middle English words and phrases. How and why has our language changed?

> Sing cuccu nu, Sing cuccu!
> Sing cuccu, Sing cuccu nu!
>
> Sumer is i-cumen in–
>   Lhude sing, cuccu!
> Groweth sed and bloweth med
>   And springth the wude nu.
>   Sing cuccu!
>
> Awe bleteth after lomb,
>   Lhouth after calve cu,
> Bulluc sterteth, bucke verteth.
>   Murie sing cuccu!
>   Cuccu, cuccu.
> Wel singes thu, cuccu.
> Ne swik thu naver nu!
>
> Sing cuccu nu, Sing cuccu!
> Sing cuccu, Sing cuccu nu!

MIDDLE ENGLISH	MODERN ENGLISH
Lhude	loud
med	meadow
awe	ewe
Lhouth after calve cu	the cow lows after her calf
Bulluc sterteth, bucke verteth	Baby bull leaps up and the buck snorts
Murie	Merrily
Ne swik	Nor ceases

41. Music was important to people on the prairie. Ask the music teacher to help you find composers who were well known at the end of the nineteenth century, for example, Stephen Foster, John Philip Sousa, or Victor Herbert. Religious songs, such as "Simple Gifts," which was written in Maine, were also popular.

42. The Great Plains was home to thousands of Native Americans before Europeans claimed the land. Read legends of Great Plains tribes, such as the Dakota Sioux, in Caduto and Bruchac's *Keepers of the Earth*. Each legend is accompanied by many science activities.

Fig. 1.9. Native Tribes of the Midwest.

43. Sarah finds a wildflower called Indian paintbrush when she is gathering wildflowers. Tomie dePaola tells how the plant got its name in *The Legend of the Indian Paintbrush*.

44. If you like stories about the prairie, try *Incident at Hawk's Hill,* by Allan W. Eckert. It is the story of a small boy and a woodchuck on the Canadian prairie.

45. Diane Siebert captures the feeling of the Great Plains in a long poem called *Heartland*. Join other students to present sections of the poem as a dramatic reading.

46. Videos can show the life of the prairie. A series by National Geographic, called Land of the Eagle, features a program called "The Prairie." For information call (800) 368-2728 or (800) 687-5060.

47. *Sarah, Plain and Tall* was produced as a TV movie. A video of the movie can be obtained from Permabound Publications, or you might be able to rent it from a local video store. The follow-up presentation was *Skylark.*

48. Celebrate the end of the unit on *Sarah, Plain and Tall* by having a Prairie Picnic. Serve only foods that farm families could produce or buy at a general store, for example, breads with sliced meats, jams, pickles and other preserves, wild berries, pies, cakes, cookies, milk, lemonade, root beer, and homemade ice cream. (Note: Root beer was a homemade product.)

Related Titles

Abbott, R. Tucker. *Seashells of the World.* Ed. by Herbert S. Zim. Golden Guide Series. New York: Golden Press, 1985.

Caduto, Michael J., and Joseph Bruchac. *Keepers of the Earth: Native American Stories & Environmental Activities for Children.* Golden, CO: Fulcrum, 1988.

Chadwick, Douglas. "Roots of the Sky." *National Geographic* 184, no. 4 (October 1993): 90-119.

dePaola, Tomie. *The Legend of the Indian Paintbrush.* New York: Putnam Pub Group, 1988.

Eckert, Allan W. *Incident at Hawk's Hill.* New York: Bantam, 1987.

Farney, Dennis. "The Tallgrass Prairie: Can It Be Saved?" *National Geographic* 157, no. 1 (January 1980): 37-61.

Gosner, Kenneth. *A Field Guide to the Atlantic Seashore.* Peterson Field Guide Series. Boston, MA: Houghton Mifflin, 1982.

Siebert, Diane. *Heartland.* New York: Crowell, 1989.

Chapter 2

The Arid Environment

Blue Willow
Doris Gates
New York: Viking, 1940

Summary

Blue Willow is set in the dry, hot, windy environment of California's San Joaquin Valley. It is the story of a Texas family, displaced by the dust storms of the 1930s, that finds employment in the valley's vast, irrigated cotton fields. The daughter of migrant workers, Janey Larkin has difficulty adjusting to her ever-changing life; she longs for a permanent home and school. The only possession she values is a blue willow plate, which signifies the stability for which she longs. She and her friend Lupe, an Hispanic girl, experience the frustrations and triumphs of early adolescence and become involved in adventures that improve the lives of both families.

Earth Concepts

Climate, weather, arid environment and rainfall, effect of wind and mountains on land, soil, seasons, rivers and sloughs

Environmental Concepts

Irrigation, cotton cultivation, agriculture, effect of temperature and rainfall on the lives of people, dust bowl and human migration

General Concepts

Bird migrations, migrant workers, cultural diversity, subsistence living, family relationships, comparison of educational settings

Activities

1. Janey and her family lived in the San Joaquin Valley of southern California. Find the valley on a map. What mountains form the valley?

Fig. 2.1. Outline Map of California.

2. Much of the San Joaquin Valley is irrigated with water from the Sacramento River. On a map follow the path of the Sacramento River as it flows south. What is the source of the river? Into what body of water does it flow? Why are there so many canals and aqueducts in this area? Check in the library media center for information on various ways to irrigate land.

3. As you read *Blue Willow,* note the various types of vegetation mentioned. Plants that grow on the flat land differ markedly from plants that grow along the rivers. How do the plants differ? Why? Do plants in your area differ depending on their proximity to water? Be sure to include trees in your analysis.

4. Why is the desert hot? Does it really get cold at night? Try this experiment in the classroom using three small, plastic, heat-resistant dishes.

   a. In the first dish put an inch of soil. In the second dish put an inch of sand. In the third dish put an inch of water.

   b. Position the dishes under a heat lamp. Measure the temperature of the substance in each dish every 60 seconds for 10 minutes.

   c. Turn off the heat lamp. Continue to measure the temperature of each substance every 60 seconds for 10 more minutes.

   d. Chart or graph the temperatures for each substance. Compare them. What conclusions can you draw about heating and cooling? How does this affect people's lives?

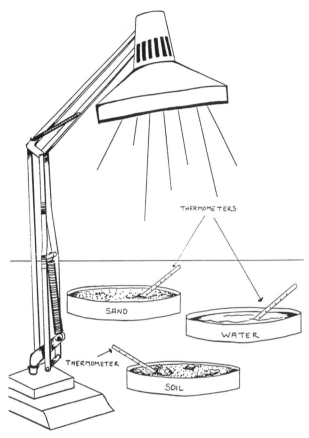

Fig. 2.2. Effect of Heat on Soils.

5. An alkali flat results when a large quantity of water evaporates from soil that is high in alkali. This process leaves dissolved minerals, such as soda and salt, on top of the soil. These flats can be as large as a pond or lake and are found in arid climates. To simulate this phenomenon, try the following experiment.

   a. Dissolve two tablespoons of baking soda or table salt in half a cup of water.

   b. Pour a little of the solution on a nonmetal or Teflon coated cookie sheet or flat baking pan.

   c. Observe how the water leaves a residue after it evaporates.

   d. To observe the effect of the hot sun, repeat this experiment with two more pans. Put one pan in the shade and put the other in the sun. How do the results differ?

6. When houseplants are not repotted for some time, a crust of minerals may form around the rim of the pot. These minerals have leached out of the soil. For more information about this topic, read "Acid Basics" by Angel Sullivan in *Science and Children* (volume 27, number 2, October 1989).

7. Cotton is one of the San Joaquin Valley's major crops.

   a. Display clothing and other items made of 100 percent cotton. Include items that show the various types of fabrics and items that can be made from cotton, for example, T-shirts, sweaters, dresses, and towels.

   b.   Use a hand lens to observe the fibers of various cotton fabrics. Do you see spaces between the fibers? Materials that contain many spaces between the fibers are good insulators. Compare cotton to wool, linen, rayon, polyester, and other synthetic fabrics.

8.   The *World Almanac* is one source of data about cotton production in the United States. Make a bar graph that shows each state's cotton production in thousands of bales. Make a second graph for cottonseed production. If almanacs for successive years are available, graph the production of cotton and cottonseed year by year.

9.   Using information from the *World Almanac,* color cotton-producing states on an outline map of the United States. Is there a pattern? Do the states have a similar climate? Refer to a social studies book to learn which states produced cotton before the Civil War. Has the pattern shifted? What does this tell you?

10.   Study the grocery store advertisements in the food and cooking section of a newspaper. As a class, predict which foods were grown in California. Then choose a small group of students to interview the produce manager of a local grocery store to see if your predictions are correct. Does the store sell other foods from California, for example, raisins? Study the advertisements from several grocery stores to compare the prices of foods from California. If some of the foods are unfamiliar, hold a tasting party to try them out.

Fig. 2.3. Produce from California.

11.   What do we mean when we say that foods are in season or not in season?

12. After you have researched the various crops and products of California, work in groups to write and produce an advertisement for a specific product. Your advertisement can be an artistic presentation or a media production. Remember that you must make your product attractive to consumers so they will buy it.

13. Adobe bricks are used for their insulating qualities. You can make adobe bricks by combining moist clay with a little straw to reinforce the clay during drying. Use natural clay dug from the ground. Knead the clay with a little water until it is the consistency of biscuit dough—moist enough to be pliable but dry enough to hold a shape. Then add the straw and knead it into the body of clay. Put the mixture into small milk cartons from which the top and opening spout have been cut. Dry the bricks in the sun or a warm part of the room until they are dry to the touch. Carefully peel the carton off each brick. To be sure the bricks are dried thoroughly, let them set for a few days before handling. NOTE: If natural clay cannot be dug, craft shops can supply powdered, potter's clay.

14. Blue Willow is a famous ceramic design that features intricate paintings in blue on a white dish. Blue Willow refers to the style; the paintings and manufacturers vary. If possible, borrow some Blue Willow pieces from a friend or relative and show them to the class. If you cannot find any Blue Willow dishes, ask the library media specialist to find some books that show Blue Willow dishes and tell about the style.

15. Farmers in the San Joaquin Valley depend heavily on migrant workers to work in the fields. Ask the library media specialist to help you learn about the life of these people. Cesar Chavez, who died in 1993, is famous for his work with the migrant workers of California. You may learn more about him by reading the biographies titled *Cesar Chavez* by Consuelo Rodriguez (Chelsea House, 1991), Ruth Franchere (Harper & Row, 1990), and David Goodwin (Fawcett, 1991).

16. Fresno, California, is the home of many Hispanic people. Read about their lives in Gary DeSoto's *Baseball in April and Other Stories* (Harcourt Brace Jovanovich, 1990).

17. *Mohave* (Harper & Row, 1988) and *Sierra* (Harper & Row, 1991), both by Diane Siebert, are beautifully illustrated poems that will give you insight into the landforms near the locale of *Blue Willow*.

18. For a recent account of life in the San Joaquin Valley, see "California: Harvest of Change" in *National Geographic* (volume 179, number 2, February 1991).

19. California is the world leader in the production of wind power. In the past, windmills needed large blades to catch the wind, and ship sails were wrapped around the axle. Modern windmills are of two types, horizontal or vertical axis. The more common horizontal axis machine is, in its basic structure, much like a traditional windmill, that is, it has a horizontal axis and vertical blades. However, modern horizontal axis machines have long, thin, propeller-like blades; a tail on the back of the machine balances the weight of the blades at the front. Horizontal axis machines must be placed on high towers. They can accept wind from only one direction at a time, so they must be able to swing around to catch wind from various directions. The second type of windmill, the vertical axis machine, has an axle that sticks straight up from the ground. The "blade of the windmill" is a large oval ring that rotates around the axle.

 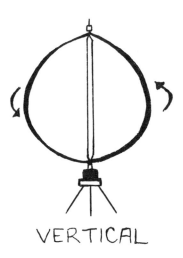

HORIZONTAL   VERTICAL

Fig. 2.4. Horizontal and Vertical Axis Windmills.

20. Build a model windmill.

   a. Use oak tag, popsicle sticks, soda straws, bamboo skewers, toothpicks, or other materials to build working models of each type of wind machine.

   b. What characteristics does a good windmill have? Compare the models to determine which has the most desirable characteristics.

21. Use the information in Table 2.1 to make graphs that show the amount of wind power generated in various parts of the world. What conclusions can you draw from the graphs you have made?

   Table 2.1 Data for Wind Generation

Place	Wind Power Generated (in millions of kilowatts)
Altamont Pass, CA	1100
Tehachapi Pass, CA	800
San Gorgonio Pass, CA	600
Denmark	500
The Netherlands	50
Hawaii	35
All others	120

22. Information about wind power is available from the American Wind Energy Association, 777 N. Capitol St., N.E., Suite 805, Washington, DC 20002.

23. Read the weather data in Table 2.2 to get an idea of the climate in the Fresno, California, area. Make a graph template: Draw the vertical axis and horizontal axis, and mark them off with 12 marks each. Label the horizontal axis with the months of the year. Make six copies of the template, and graph each weather feature on a different graph. For example, on the first graph label the vertical axis "Average Daily High Temperature, Degrees

Fahrenheit," and label the marks 50, 55, 60, 65, and so forth. On the second graph, label the vertical axis "Clear Days," and number the marks 3, 6, 9, and so forth. Copy the graphs onto transparencies and lay one over the other to compare the data.

You can do many other activities with this data:

a. For each weather feature, list the months in rank order, from highest to lowest. For example, for the average daily high temperature, begin the list with the month that had the highest temperature and end it with the month that had the lowest temperature.

b. Compare the weather features of one month to another. For example, compare the relative humidity of the month with the highest temperature to the relative humidity of the month with the lowest temperature.

c. Write weather reports based on the data in the weather table. For example, to write a weather report for Valentine's Day (or any day in February), use the data given for February.

d. Compare the climate of Fresno to the climate in your community.

e. Form groups to challenge each other to answer questions about the data, for example

Why does the humidity drop in the afternoon?

Why are there many more clear days in the summer?

How does the wind affect the people?

Table 2.2 Weather Data for Fresno, California

Month	Jan	Feb	Mar	Apr	May	Jun	Jul	Aug	Sep	Oct	Nov	Dec
average daily high temp	56	59	69	79	82	92	99	95	91	84	67	53
clear days per month	8	12	13	8	14	28	28	24	25	24	18	18
relative humidity at 10 am	86	70	63	53	43	38	36	43	43	39	53	76
relative humidity at 4 pm	64	51	44	35	31	23	24	28	27	28	36	50
Total precipitation per month (inch)	2.8	1.3	.67	.92	1.6	0	0	0	.15	.05	.46	.68
wind (mph)	4.4	6.1	5.4	7.0	7.9	8.6	7.8	7.5	6.1	4.2	3.6	3.3

Source: Weather Data for Fresno, California. National Oceanic and Atmospheric Administration, Washington, D.C., 1990.

24. Foggy mornings are often mentioned in the book. Table 2.3 lists the average number of foggy days, with visibility of a quarter mile or less, for Fresno, California. Discuss the data and suggest reasons why fog might be so common from November through February.

Table 2.3 Foggy Days in Fresno, California

Foggy Days	11.7	6.0	1.8	0.4	0.1	0	0	0	0.1	0.9	6.1	12.2

Source: Weather Data for Fresno, California. National Oceanic and Atmospheric Administration, Washington, D.C., 1990.

25. To demonstrate the conditions under which fog is caused, try the following experiment.

   a. Place a small amount of warm water in a clear plastic tumbler. Cover the tumbler tightly with plastic wrap.

   b. Place ice cubes on top of the plastic wrap.

   c. Observe cloudiness forming in the tumbler. How do the conditions in the tumbler resemble those on the ground and in the air in the winter near Fresno, California?

26. Sand is common in arid areas. Ask friends or family members who live in other communities to send you a small sample of sand in a sealed plastic bag. Ask them to attach a label indicating where the sand was collected. Use a hand lens to examine the samples for color, luster, texture, and composition.

27. Using disposable plates, design a china pattern. Plastic and styrofoam plates are more durable than paper plates, but if you use plastic or styrofoam, you may have to glue your design onto the plate. You may preserve the design with spray varnish, if the varnish won't ruin the design.

28. Use cotton balls and natural items, such as seeds, twigs, or leaves, to create a three-dimensional work of art. The cotton balls can be gently pulled into various shapes, exposing their fibers.

Fig. 2.5. Art Projects Using Natural Materials.

29. Janey used sunflowers to measure the progress of the seasons of the year. What plants or trees in your neighborhood change with the seasons? What plants remain somewhat the same throughout the year?

30. Sunflowers have many uses. In the library media center, research their various uses. Make a bulletin board display of large paper sunflowers; on each bloom write a different use for the plant. Make a second bulletin board to show the uses of the cotton plant. Compare the plants' uses.

31. The Larkin family left Texas because of a drought, which produced an area known as the Dust Bowl. Investigate this phenomenon, which began in the 1930s. In what part of the country are droughts common today? What effect does this have on the people who live there? How are others affected? How would your life change if the amount of rainfall suddenly began to decrease each year?

32. One of the most famous singers and songwriters of the Dust Bowl era was Woodie Guthrie. You have probably sung his song "This Land Is Your Land." Ask your music teacher to help you find other songs by Woodie Guthrie.

33. The cotton picking contest was one of the highlights of the year for Janey and Lupe. It was widely advertised and offered prizes to the winners. With your class sponsor a contest. Decide a purpose for the contest, set a date, distribute advertisements, select contestants, choose judges, stage the contest, and award prizes. Your contest could be a science fair or social studies fair based on *Blue Willow,* or it could be a noncompetitive contest in which everyone who reads a certain number of books in a month wins a prize.

Related Titles

DeSoto, Gary. *Baseball in April and Other Stories*. San Diego, CA: Harcourt Brace Jovanovich, 1990.

Ellis, William S. "California: Harvest of Change." *National Geographic* 179, no. 2 (February 1991): 49-73.

Franchere, Ruth. *Cesar Chavez*. New York: Harper & Row, 1990.

Goodwin, David. *Cesar Chavez*. New York: Fawcett, 1991.

Rodriguez, Consuelo. *Cesar Chavez*. New York: Chelsea House, 1991.

Siebert, Diane. *Mohave*. New York: Harper & Row, 1988.

———. *Sierra*. New York: Harper & Row, 1991.

Sullivan, Angel. "Acid Basics." *Science and Children* 27, no. 2 (October 1989): 22-24.

Chapter 3
Tornadoes and Weather

Night of the Twisters

Ivy Ruckman
New York: HarperCollins, 1986

Summary

On June 4, 1980, a series of tornadoes devastated the city of Grand Island, Nebraska. This novel tells the story of the tornadoes and their aftermath through a first person account of a young boy. The narrative begins several hours before the storm hits. As the storm nears, Danny's parents leave him with his baby brother and go to warn relatives. Danny and his best friend, Arthur, ensure their own safety and, after the storm, find their families. Stacy, Arthur's sister, finds them after they leave the destroyed house.

Earth Concepts

Weather; atmosphere; tornadoes—description, cause, and effect; conditions that spawn tornadoes; warning signs of tornadoes; air and water pressure; geography of Nebraska

Environmental Concepts

Destruction of man-made environment by natural forces, power of nature, relationship of people to the environment

General Concepts

Preparing for a storm, survival, reactions of people to disaster, aftermath of a disaster, reconstructing a way of life

Activities

1. A good definition of *tornado* appears in the *World Almanac*. The almanac also lists places hit by the country's worst tornadoes.

   a. On an outline map of the United States, indicate where the worst tornadoes have hit. Be sure to indicate the tornado in Grand Island, Nebraska. Study the map to draw conclusions about tornadoes.

b. After you indicate where the worst tornadoes have hit, color in the states that experience the greatest number of tornadoes. Use a color code, for example, red for states with 0–5 tornadoes per year, blue for states with 6–10 tornadoes per year, and so forth.

2. On a landform map of the United States or Nebraska obtained from the library media center, locate Grand Island and the Platte River. Describe the topography of the state. What does the topography tell you about why tornadoes travel so easily in the Midwest? Compare the topography of Nebraska to the topography of the area in which you live. Look for pictures of Nebraska in your social studies book or in the library media center.

Fig. 3.1. Outline Map of Nebraska.

3. On June 3, 1980, weather forecasters predicted a 20 percent chance of showers for Grand Island, Nebraska. But the weather was quite different. Arthur and Danny noticed strange weather signs in the afternoon and evening before the tornado hit. What signs suggested that something unusual was going to happen? Make a chart that shows the warning signs and the precautions taken for each hour preceding the tornado. Use the following chart as a pattern.

Time Line of *Night of the Twisters*

	Warning signs	Precautions
3 p.m.		
4 p.m.		
5 p.m.		
7 p.m.		
8 p.m.		
9 p.m.		

4. The first of several tornadoes hit shortly after 9 p.m. If you were a reporter for the 11 p.m. news, you would have a very difficult time filing a complete report by 10:30 p.m. Roads would be impassable and telephone lines would be down. What information would you be able to gather for your 10:30 p.m. report? In addition to the little you could observe, what sources of information would you rely upon? Are all sources of information reliable?

5. Role play the parts of Danny, Arthur, and Stacy as they seek their parents. Show how they would act and what they would say to a reporter. What would the reporter ask them? Role play interviews with Arthur's and Danny's mothers before they are reunited with their families.

6. The National Weather Service provides national and regional forecasts to newspapers throughout the United States. Figure 3.2 shows weather maps for the week of May 28 through June 3, 1980.

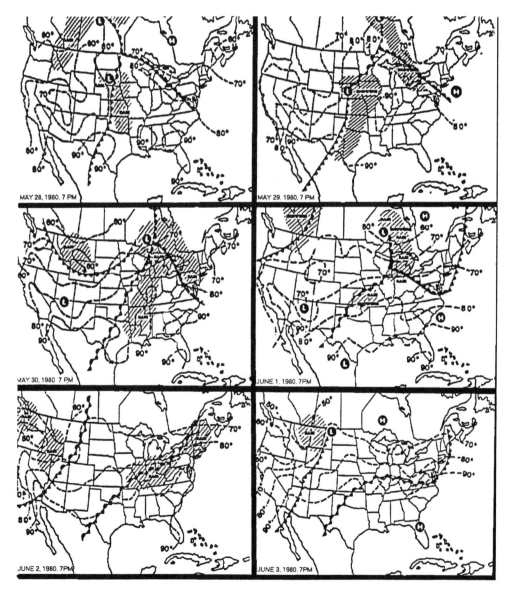

Fig. 3.2. Weather Maps for Week of May 28, 1980. Source: National Weather Service.

Study the sequence of events in the maps. How did the weather change in Nebraska during that week? Were there any signs of an approaching tornado or violent weather pattern? What was the prediction for Grand Island on June 3? What was the weather like on that day in other cities, such as San Francisco, Miami, Portland, Maine, Chicago, Denver, Seattle, and Atlanta? What was the weather pattern where you live on that date?

7. Look at a weather map in your local newspaper. Check the key to learn what basic weather symbols mean. Learn the symbols for temperature, air pressure, frontal systems, precipitation, wind direction, and other events or features.

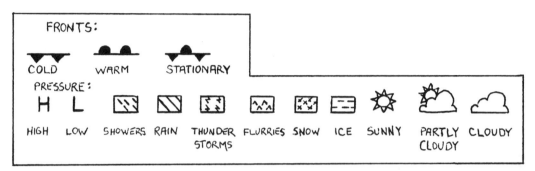

Fig. 3.3. Weather Symbols.

8. Collect weather maps from your local newspaper for a week. Cut out the maps and place them in order on a sheet of paper. Pick a low pressure area in the western part of the United States and observe how it moves across the country each day. Do this for other high pressure or low pressure areas or storms. Check the direction of the wind and its relation to the weather. For example, winter winds from Canada are usually followed by cold weather. Do the maps indicate other movements? Where do fronts and weather patterns eventually go?

9. If possible, ask a weather forecaster or meteorologist to speak to your class about the kinds of storms that occur in your area and how they are predicted. What instruments are used to predict the weather? What other sources of information are used, for example, information from the National Weather Service? What part do weather satellites play in local weather prediction? How accurate are weather and storm predictions?

10. Talk about the precautions you would take before an impending storm. List general supplies that everyone would need, such as water, flashlights, and blankets. Add items your family would need, for example, medicines or diapers. If you had to stay in a community shelter, what other things would you take, perhaps a teddy bear for a young child? [Teacher's note: This activity may upset some children; modify it to suit your students.]

11. If a severe storm or disaster warning were issued while you were in school, you would follow school safety guidelines. Find out from the principal or another administrator what those guidelines are. How would a real emergency differ from a practice session like a fire drill? What provisions are made for students whose parents work or students who go to after-school programs?

12. Using *Night of the Twisters* and your own knowledge, work with your class to create an emergency plan. Stage a mock emergency to test the plan. On a large map of your community block out an area to indicate where the mock tornado hit. Role play government officials, police, firefighters, road crews, emergency medical crews, hospital staff, utilities staff, news reporters, and private citizens. Include the following in your drill.

   a. Check transportation capabilities: be sure streets are clear and evacuation routes are in order.

   b. Organize relief efforts, including locating large halls to house people and sources of food, water, blankets, and medical supplies.

   c. Contact sources of help, such as the National Guard or Red Cross.

   d. Inform the public of what has happened, the progress being made in clearing roads and restoring services, and efforts being made to help locate family members, and so on.

   e. Assess damage to public service facilities—police station, radio station, etc.

   f. Assess damage to public utilities, such as water, sewer, electricity or gas, and telephone.

   g. Think of other persons or organizations to call upon for help and think of situations in which people need help for specific problems, for example, kidney dialysis patients who have lost their water service.

13. Discuss other situations in which an impending storm would force you to take emergency actions. What would you do if a severe storm warning were announced when you were at the mall? At the movies? Playing outside? At a friend's house? Remember, you must seek shelter quickly to insure your safety. Going home might not be an option.

14. Many natural or man-made emergencies can disrupt our lives. We need to be prepared to deal with them. What would you need to cope with the loss of electricity for several hours or even days? What if the water were shut off for an indefinite period of time? Think of other situations in which you might have to help your family as Danny and Arthur did in *Night of the Twisters*.

Fig. 3.4. Formation of a Tornado.

15. Simulate a tornado by creating a vortex in a soft drink bottle. Try this method or the method described in activity 16. This method is called Tornado in a Bottle.

    a. Fill a 2-liter bottle with water, leaving a 2 inch airspace at the top.

    b. Add one teaspoon of salt.

    c. Add a tiny drop of clear dishwashing liquid. (Too much soap will ruin the effect.)

    d. Put tiny pieces of stone, wood, and other debris in the bottle. Let them sink to the bottom.

    e. Cap the bottle and rotate it counterclockwise. When the rotation is fast enough, a vortex will form.

Fig. 3.5. Tornado in a Bottle.

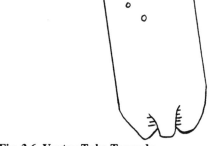

16. Use a tornado vortex tube to simulate a tornado in a soda bottle.

    a. From a museum gift shop or science supply store or catalog purchase a plastic tube threaded at both ends. Be sure it is the right size to screw onto a 2-liter soda bottle.

    b. Fill one bottle two-thirds full of water.

    c. Screw the tube onto the soda bottle that contains the water. Turn the second soda bottle upside down and screw it onto the other end of the tube.

    d. Turn the tornado tube upside down so that the bottle containing the water is on top.

    e. As the water drains from the top bottle into the bottom one, it forms a vortex. Notice the direction in which it turns.

Fig. 3.6. Vortex Tube Tornado.

17. You can do several interesting demonstrations of air and water pressure using 2-liter soda bottles.

    a. Set out a pail of hot water and a pail of ice water. Immerse the bottom half of an empty, uncapped 2-liter soda bottle in hot water for several minutes. Do not let any water get into the bottle or on your hand. Cap the bottle and immerse the bottom half of it in ice water for several minutes. What happens to the air pressure inside the bottle as it cools? What evidence shows there is a pressure change? What happens if you remove the cap and reheat the bottle?

    b. Fit the neck of a balloon over the mouth of an empty 2-liter soda bottle. Immerse the bottom half of the bottle in hot water for several minutes. Observe as the air pressure and temperature in the bottle increase. Remove the bottle and hold it up in the air. What happens to the balloon as the bottle cools? Why?

18. Wind patterns are caused by a combination of the heating and cooling of air and the rotation of the Earth. The speed and duration of the wind generated depends on the amount of heating and cooling. Figure 3.7 shows a map of prevailing wind currents on the Earth. Determine from which direction various winds normally blow. Check your home; Grand Island, Nebraska; Sidney, Australia; Point Barrow, Alaska; Honolulu; Paris; Cairo; Beijing; and other places you have studied or visited.

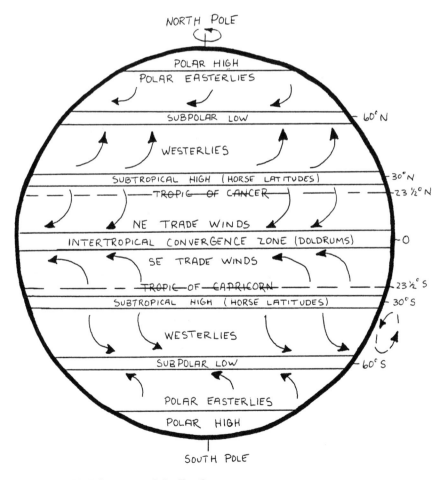

Fig. 3.7. Wind Currents of the Earth.

19. The Beaufort Scale (see table 3.1) provides an easy way to estimate wind speed. The scale, described in the following table, is based on familiar occurrences, such as rising smoke. Every day for at least one week, go to the school yard to observe and estimate wind speed. Make your observations at the same time every day. Compile a classroom log that compares wind speed and direction to cloud cover and precipitation.

Table 3.1 The Beaufort Scale

Force	Strength	MPH	Effect
0	Calm	0–1	Smoke rises vertically
1	Light air	1–3	Smoke drifts slowly to the side
2	Light breeze	4–7	Wind felt on face
3	Gentle breeze	7–12	Light flag unfurls
4	Moderate breeze	12–18	Paper blows about
5	Fresh breeze	19–24	Small trees move
6	Strong breeze	25–31	Umbrellas turn inside out
7	Near gale	32–38	Difficult to walk against wind
8	Gale	39–46	Twigs break off trees
9	Strong gale	47–54	Branches blow down
10	Storm	55–63	Trees uprooted
11	Violent storm	63–73	Widespread building damage
12	Hurricane	>74	Devastation

20. Many tools are used to record weather data. For example, rain can be measured in a tall, thin bottle or glass, and wind direction can be detected with a windsock and compass. These tools can be made using common materials as shown on page 33.

21. Indoors or outdoors, you are constantly surrounded by wind in the form of air currents. The currents are too feeble to move a windsock but can be detected with a little smoke. You can detect currents by lighting a piece of incense in an incense burner. The smoldering incense produces a thin column of smoke, which is deflected by air currents. Test the air currents at several heights. Doors, windows, and radiators or air conditioners make especially interesting currents. Record the information you gather in three-dimensional charts. Explain air movement in the classroom.

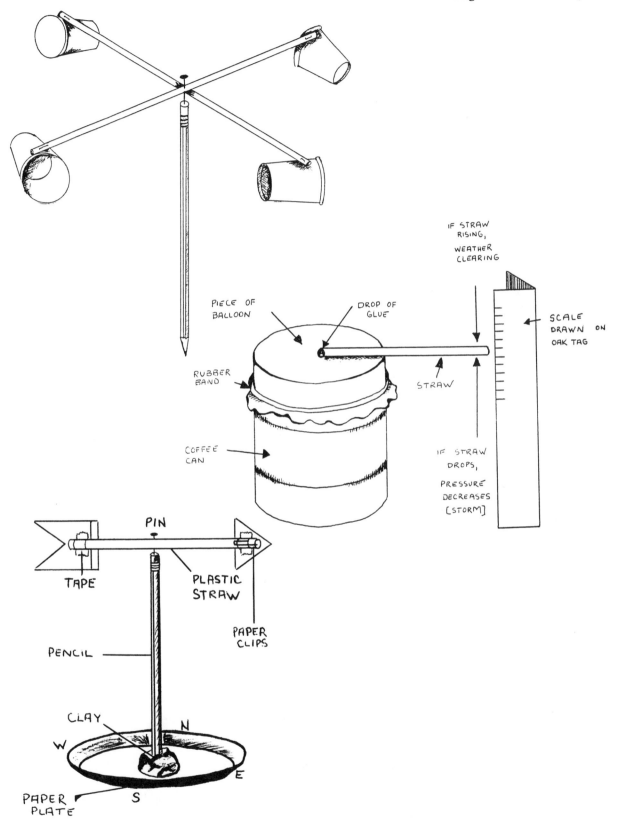

IF STRAW
RISING,
WEATHER
CLEARING

PIECE OF
BALLOON

DROP OF
GLUE

SCALE
DRAWN ON
OAK TAG

RUBBER
BAND

STRAW

COFFEE
CAN

IF STRAW
DROPS,
PRESSURE
DECREASES
[STORM]

PIN

TAPE

PLASTIC
STRAW

PAPER
CLIPS

PENCIL

CLAY

N

W

E

S

PAPER
PLATE

Fig. 3.8. Weather Instruments: From Top to Bottom—Wind Speed, Barometric Pressure, Wind Direction.

22. Your class can map the air currents outside the school by recording the drift of bubbles made with bubble wands and a soap solution. Carefully observe near corners, vents, doors, and windows. Does the height from the ground affect how the air moves? Is air movement the same on all sides of the building? From which direction does the wind appear to come?

   To make bubbles, combine

   ¼ cup glycerine (available in drug stores)

   ¼ cup Joy or Dawn dishwashing liquid

   2 cups water

   For best results, mix and let stand overnight before using.

23. *Roget's Thesaurus* gives many synonyms for *wind,* for example, breeze, whiff, puff, draft, zephyr, stream, flurry, tempest, current, gust, storm, gale, blizzard, blast, squall, hurricane, whirlwind, cyclone, tornado, and twister. Which winds are very gentle? Which are the strongest? Which flow in a particular pattern? List the types of wind from the most gentle to the most violent. Compare your list with your classmates' lists. Do you all agree on the order? Use some of the synonyms to write descriptions or poetry about the wind.

24. Few of us will ever experience a storm like the one described in *Night of the Twisters,* but we have experienced various kinds of storms. Describe a storm that you experienced: how it began, what it was like, what you did during the storm, how it ended, what happened afterward. You may describe the whole storm or pick one part that affected you most.

25. Acronyms are descriptive words or phrases made from the first letter of a series of words. For example, the acronym MADD stands for Mothers Against Drunk Driving. Acronyms can be creative, and you can even write poems with them. A poetic interpretation of the acronym TWISTER might be

   Temperature rising

   Wind gusting

   Ice forming

   Storm warnings

   Tornado striking

   Electricity zig-zagging

   Rain torrents beating down

   Write your own poetic acronyms for words from *Night of the Twisters,* such as rain, air, hail, lightning, clouds, explosion, storm, fire, wind, thunder, humidity, flood, heat, or the names of some characters in the story.

26. Descriptions acquire added meaning when they compare an unfamiliar object or feeling to a familiar one. One way to do this is to use a simile, a comparison that uses *like* or *as.* Write some similes about wind or the effect of wind, for example, "His bedroom looked like a tornado had gone through it" or "Even a slight draft was as chilling as an ice cube when she was reading the horror story."

27. Based on what you read in *Night of the Twisters,* how would you describe the tornado and its effect on the houses and the environment? Make a bulletin board display of cards, with each card bearing one idea about the storm, for example, "It shatters windows" or "It is faster than a speeding car." Ask the library media specialist to help you find pictures of tornadoes or their aftermath to illustrate your bulletin board.

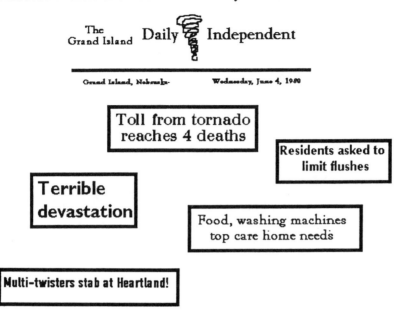

Fig. 3.9. Tornado News Headlines—Grand Island, Nebraska.

28. The American Red Cross provides checklists and instructions to help you prepare for storms. Call or write your local chapter office to ask for publications titled "Your Family Disaster Supplies Kit," "Weather from Behind the Wheel," and "Plan and Get Ready." Ask whether the local chapter office has any information written for your area.

29. It takes months to clean up the debris after a tornado hits. Look around your room for some debris, or discards, that can be used in art projects. Small items that can be glued to paper or to each other work best.

    a. Make a junk collage: Glue small discards, such as old keys, broken combs, bottle caps, pieces of old toys, or cassette tapes to pieces of cardboard. After the glue dries, spray paint the entire piece for a dazzling effect.

    b. Make a junk mobile: Tie small pieces of junk to a wire coat hanger, making sure that different pieces hang at different lengths. Monofilament nylon will make it look like the items are suspended in space.

    c. Make a junk sculpture: Create a sculpture from paper and styrofoam. Use small boxes, pizza cartons, tissue rolls, egg cartons, newspaper, and other scrap materials. Affix the sculpture to a base so that it can be displayed.

Fig. 3.10. Junk Collage.

30. For other ideas about using recycled materials for art projects, see *Good Earth Art* by Mary Ann Kohl and Cindy Gainer (Mt. Rainier, MD: Gryphon House).

31. One excellent article on the setting of *Night of the Twisters* is "Nebraska's Sand Hills," which appeared in *National Geographic* (volume 154, number 4, October 1978). Look for the article in your library media center's collection of back copies of *National Geographic*. The article offers many photographs of the Nebraska landscape. Locate the city of Grand Island and the North Platte River.

Related Titles

Kohl, Mary Ann, and Cindy Gainer. *Good Earth Art*. Mt. Rainier, MD: Gryphon House, 1991.

Madson, John. "Nebraska's Sand Hills." *National Geographic* 154, no. 4 (October 1978): 493-517.

Chapter 4

The Arctic

Julie of the Wolves
Jean Craighead George
New York: Harper & Row, 1972

Summary

Julie, a young Inuit girl, is forced into an early marriage with a dull-witted boy named Daniel. Unable to accept this fate, she leaves Barrow, Alaska, to seek her pen pal's home in San Francisco. She becomes lost for several months on the North Slope, but she survives with the help of a wolf pack and her own knowledge of the tundra and arctic environment. Eventually she is reunited with her father, but even then she must resolve the inner conflict between the modern world and traditional Eskimo values.

Earth Concepts

Arctic climate, tundra and permafrost, characteristics of snow, seasons, landforms, geography of Alaska, astronomy, celestial navigation

Environmental Concepts

Management of trash and refuse, effect of an oil pipeline on an environment, food chain, animal behavior, adaptation to many hours of dark in winter, wolf myths and facts

General Concepts

Inuit culture and customs, survival, conflict of traditional and modern values, adolescence, animal communication, bounties on animals

Activities

1. Using a map of Alaska, find the area in which the story takes place by locating the Brooks Range, the Arctic Ocean, the Beaufort Sea, Nunivak Island, Point Hope, and Barrow. Trace Julie's journey using clues from the book.

Fig. 4.1. Outline Map of Alaska.

2. The tundra is a land of poor soil, low temperatures, and a limited growing season. Simulate growing plants under those conditions. Use soil that is sandy and gravelly. Keep the plants in a very cool, dry place, and water them sparingly. Grow a second set of plants in fertile soil, such as potting soil, in a warm, bright environment with plenty of water. After a few weeks, compare the plants. Which appear more healthy?

3. The tundra is a fragile ecosystem. It is easily damaged by solid waste disposal, because solid waste does not decompose readily in the cold, dry conditions. Each 18-degree (Fahrenheit) drop in temperature doubles the time it takes for solid waste to decompose. When items are frozen decomposition stops. This is why remains of humans and animals have been found preserved after thousands of years in the ice. To illustrate the problem of cold-weather decomposition, compare decomposition rates under favorable conditions and under cold, dry conditions. A considerable amount of mold will be generated by this activity and could irritate students with mold allergies.

    a. Take a large, flat pan with sides about two inches high or a flat box lined with a trash bag.

    b. Spread 1 inch of soil in the container. On top of the soil place several thin layers of trash, such as scraps of newspaper, the lid of a tin can, scraps of aluminum foil, paper towels, wood shavings, cloth, plant leaves, bread, and potato peelings.

    c. Spread a layer of soil over the trash. Water the pile lightly each day.

    d. Fill an identical container with the same items and place it in a large freezer.

    e. After one month, gently dig up the trash in the warm container to observe the rate of decay. Then chip out the items in the frozen container and observe their rate of decay.

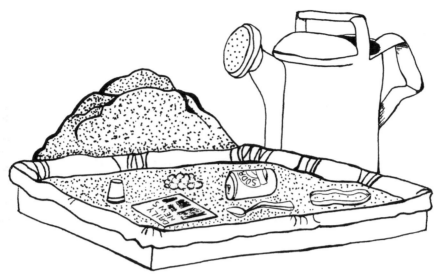

Fig. 4.2. Decomposition Activity Box.

f. Compare the decomposition that took place in each tray using a scale of 0 to 10, with 0 = no decomposition and 10 = complete decomposition.

4. In the harsh climate of the tundra, people must wear protective clothing. To show how insulation works, try this experiment.

a. Make gelatin in a flat pan and cut it into 2-inch squares. The gelatin squares represent people who must be protected from the cold.

b. Working alone or in a group, find a way to protect the gelatin from extreme cold. Insert a thermometer into the gelatin. Protect the gelatin by wrapping it in insulating materials or placing it in a container packed with insulating materials. Some insulating materials are wood chips, styrofoam, dry grass, and cloth.

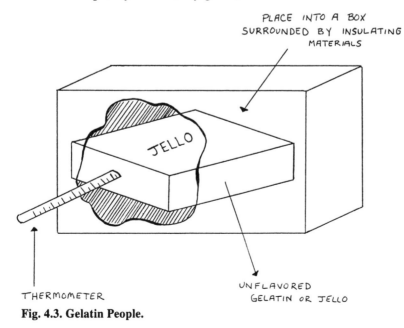

Fig. 4.3. Gelatin People.

c. Place the containers in a freezer or set them outside on a very cold day. Measure the temperature every 10 or 15 minutes, and make a graph of time versus temperature for each container. What is the best insulator? Why?

5. Julie used the stars as a guide to find her way back to her people. The following activities will help you learn about constellations.

   a. A fun way to learn some constellations is to make a deck of cards, replacing the four suits (spades, clubs, diamonds, and hearts) with four familiar constellations. Some familiar constellations are Canis Major, Orion, Cassiopeia, Ursa Minor, Ursa Major, Andromeda, Taurus, Sagittarius, Perseus, Cygnus, Leo, Hercules, Pegasus, Drago, and Cepheus. Use Polaris (the North Star) or your favorite star for the joker.

   b. Play card games, like rummy, that require players to collect three or more cards of the same suit, or constellation. Add a twist: To lay down a set of matching cards, the player must name the constellation on them.

   c. Make up versions of Go Fish!, Old Maid, War, and other card games, using constellation cards.

6. The many animals mentioned in *Julie of the Wolves* have adapted to life in the Arctic. These animals include the ptarmigan, dog, lemming, bear, walrus, wolverine, weasel, rabbit, deer, elk, snowy owl, puffin, white whale, eider duck, musk oxen, and caribou. Following are jumbled versions of those animals' names. Pick out and unscramble the capitalized letters to spell the harsh reality that Julie faced.

   gImmlen

   Leasew

   skum nOxe

   kEl

   edRe

   bRae

   tArpgmian

   saWlur

   woNys low

   fufpIn

   boariuC

   Tewih lewha

   ridee kdCu

   Tabrib

   Noweliver

   Gdo

7. Use resources in the library media center to research one or more arctic animals. Write a description of an arctic animal and make a sketch to illustrate it. Hang your work on a classroom bulletin board about arctic animals.

8. Select three or four unique characteristics of the animal you researched. Be sure the characteristics you select are unique to that animal! A white coat, for example, is not unique. Write each characteristic on a separate index card. Pick one person to shuffle the cards and to distribute one card to each student. Walk around the classroom, reading other students' clues. When you find someone holding a clue that matches your clue—that is, both of your clues belong to the same animal—stand with that person. As a pair, continue to look for one or two more students holding clues to your animal. The first group to have all the correct cards for one animal wins. Adjust the number of cards to fit the size of your class. For example, if you have 24 students, hand out only two clues for each animal or do four clues for just six of the animals.

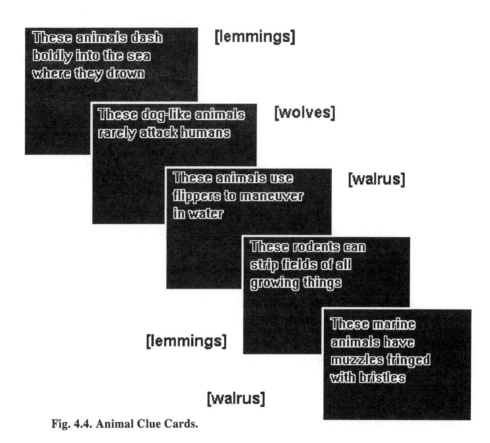

Fig. 4.4. Animal Clue Cards.

9. Julie's life was saved by the wolves. However, many people have negative feelings about the wolf. Administer the following survey (page 42) to the adults in your family. Compile the data you collect, draw conclusions about people's attitudes. You may wish to formulate some math problems such as the percentage of responses for each item.

10. Julie often speaks about signs of the approaching autumn and winter. What signs signal the change of seasons in the Arctic? Compare these signs to the signs of approaching autumn and winter in your area.

11. In the far north of Alaska the sun does not rise between November 18 and January 24. Conversely, the sun does not set between May 10 and August 2. How long are the days in your area during these periods? Use newspapers in your library media center as a source of data.

AN ATTITUDE SURVEY—THE WOLF

Age Group:
    18-25 _____
    26-42 _____
    43-50 _____
    51-58 _____
    over 59 _____

Educational Level:
    High School Graduate _____
    Some College   _____
    College Graduate   _____
    Additional College   _____

Gender:
    Male   _____
    Female _____

Directions
Mark whether you think the statement is true or false.

       T   F

1. _____ _____ Wolves usually will attack people.

2. _____ _____ The average wolf is the size of a German shepherd.

3. _____ _____ If you are bitten by a wolf you will get rabies.

4. _____ _____ Wolves travel in packs because of their strong sense of community.

5. _____ _____ Wolves howl because they are about to attack.

6. _____ _____ Wolves are a nuisance to rural communities.

7. _____ _____ The wolf population should be protected by law.

8. _____ _____ Wolves are a beneficial part of the environment.

Comments:

---

12. Consider how days of complete dark or light would affect your life. Under the headings Dark and Light list three types of activities: those that would be unchanged, those that would be completely changed, and those that would need to be modified. For example, you would catch the school bus at the same time during the dark winter, but you could play baseball at midnight in the middle of summer.

13. The Inuit, who inhabit a wide-ranging area across northern Canada and Alaska, would like to be self-governing. Study the map that shows the boundary of the proposed Inuit territory Nunavut. Why do the Inuit want to be self-governing? How would this affect Alaskan Inuit? How would their lives change? What are the natural resources of Nunavut? Are there any towns in this area? What means of transportation are used?

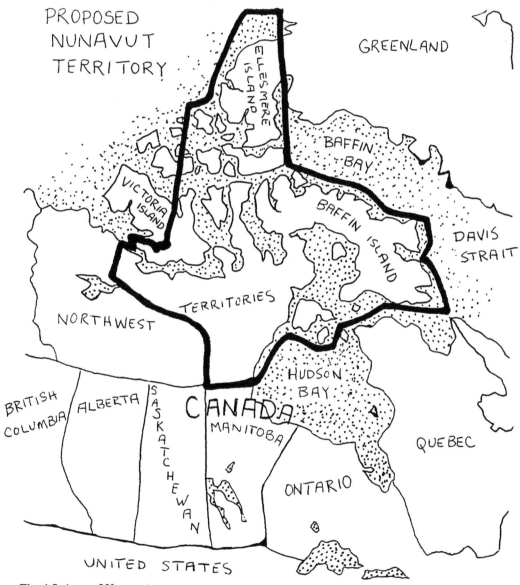

Fig. 4.5. Area of Nunavut.

14. Describe various aspects of Julie's Inuit culture by completing table 4.1. Use information from *Julie of the Wolves* and other resources in the library media center.

Table 4.1 Cultural Comparisons

Transportation	Clothing	Utensils	Housing	Food

    a. Use a similar chart to describe your own culture. Compare and contrast the two cultures, yours and Julie's. Then compare your culture to classmates' cultures. You may find some differences.

15. As you read the book, note references to what Julie eats during her journey. Note the sources of her food and the nutritional content of her diet. Compare the sources and nutritional content of Julie's diet to the food pyramid (see fig. 4.6). The food pyramid represents the United States government's recommendation for a well-balanced diet. How does Julie's diet compare to the food pyramid? How does your own diet compare?

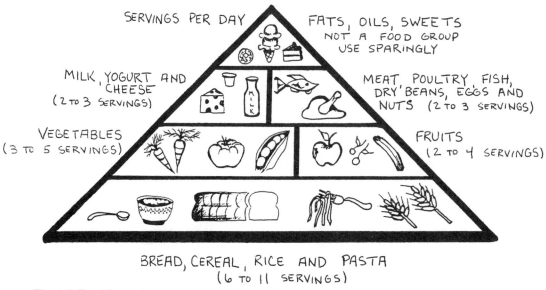

Fig. 4.6. Food Pyramid.

16. One form of Inuit art is figures of animals carved in soapstone or bone. Using white, unscented soap and plastic, serrated knives, carve an arctic animal. Save the soap chips to use later.

Fig. 4.7. Carving of an Arctic Animal.

17. After being reunited with her family, Julie may have written to her pen pal in San Francisco. Write a letter as if you were Julie and describe your journey to your friend. You may include Julie's plans for the future.

Chapter 5

The North Woods

The Incredible Journey

Sheila Burnford

New York: Bantam Books, 1961

Summary

Western Ontario, Canada, is a land of forests, marshy swamps, lakes, rivers, and streams. It is an isolated wilderness with few human inhabitants outside of scattered mining enclaves. In this environment three animals are accidentally abandoned. *The Incredible Journey* is the story of an English bulldog, a Labrador retriever, and a Siamese cat who face many natural dangers as they try to find their vacationing family.

Earth Concepts

Lakes, rivers, northern wetlands or swamps, climate and weather, mineral deposits, watersheds

Environmental Concepts

Trees and logging, mining and abuse of the land, animal and plant ecology, birds' patterns of migration, animal alterations to the environment, predator–prey relationships, animal camouflage and hibernation

General Concepts

Comparison of rural and urban Canada, isolation, animal instincts and sense of direction, geographical interpretation

Activities

1. The animals in *The Incredible Journey* cross a series of connected lakes, rivers, and streams to end up at Lake Windigo. Scientists call this a watershed. Your school yard is a watershed of sorts. Map your school yard as a class activity. After a heavy rain, use the map to record where the rain collects and where it drains. In what directions does it travel? Are there places where the water remains standing? Describe how the water affects the school yard.

2. You can map the watershed covered in *The Incredible Journey*. Figure 5.1 is a map that shows the drainage area for Lake Windigo. As smaller streams flow into larger streams, they form a **V**. The **V** usually points downstream to a larger body of water. (Note this is only true for a **V** that is formed when a smaller stream joins a larger one. When a stream splits in two, the **V** usually points upstream.) On the map trace the flow of the river from any point to another point. Notice that the flow appears to be haphazard. What does that suggest about the topography of this region? North is at the top of the map.

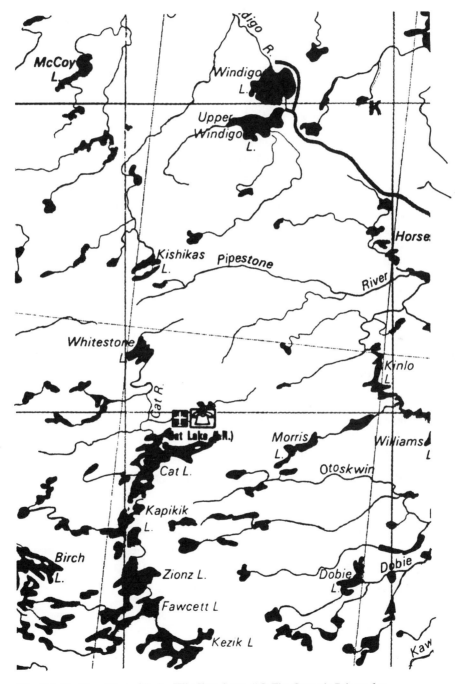

Fig. 5.1. Outline Map of Lake Windigo Area. "© The Queen's Printer for Ontario, 1994. Reproduced with permission."

3. Using a U.S. Geological Survey topographical map or a detailed map of your area, trace the paths of smaller streams into larger streams. Where does the water eventually flow? Locate several major North American rivers and trace their paths to the Atlantic Ocean, Pacific Ocean, Gulf of Mexico, or other end point.

4. The animals in *The Incredible Journey* were caught in a swiftly flowing river. You can judge the speed of a stream's flow by inspecting the streambed.

   > Flow is slow: silt

   > Flow is medium: gravel

   > Flow is rapid: large rocks

   > Flow is torrential: boulders

5. If you have a shallow stream accessible to your school, you can try this activity. It can be done using pairs of supervised students or as a demonstration.

   a. With a partner measure the speed of the stream's flow. Pick two spots on the stream bank about 50 feet apart. Have your partner stand at the downstream point with a stopwatch, and you stand at the upstream point with a small branch or other lightweight natural object. Call out "1, 2, 3, go!" and on "go!" toss the stick into the stream. Your partner will time how many seconds it takes the stick to float 50 feet.

   b. Measure the volume of water in a 50 feet stretch of the stream. On the stream bank, mark a 50 feet segment of the stream. Measure the average width and average depth within that segment. Be sure all your measurements are in feet. Calculate the volume by multiplying the length by the depth and multiplying that total by the width. Now you know the volume of that segment in cubic feet.

   c. Now you know both the speed of the flow and the volume of water in a 50-foot segment of the stream. Use these figures to state the stream's flow in cubic feet per second.

   $$\text{Volume of flow} \quad = \quad \frac{\text{Volume (from step b)}}{\text{Time (from step a)}}$$

   d. Measure the temperature and pH (acidity) of the water, and observe its clarity, color, and odor. Kits can be obtained from science supply houses to measure for pH as well as dissolved oxygen.

   e. Sketch animals and plants found in the stream. Discuss the characteristics of plants and animals found in slow-moving water as compared to plants and animals found in fast-moving water.

   f. Study the insects and small animals in and around the stream. Observe their movements and how they catch food. After you return to the classroom, take turns pantomiming the insects and animals.

   g. Use writing, artwork, and movement to answer the following questions.

      > What is the relationship of the speed of the stream's flow to the composition of the stream bottom, the water's color, and plant and animal life?

      > Do streams that flow slowly support more plant and animal life than streams that flow quickly?

      > Is the speed of the flow related to the temperature or pH?

6. Acid rain is a great concern in Ontario and other parts of the world. You can simulate its effects in the classroom using an acidic solution of white vinegar and water.

    a. Plant fast-growing plants like beans or radishes. Divide the plantings into four groups.

    b. Water the first group with tap water.

    c. Water the second group with a solution of 1 part white vinegar and 1 part water.

    d. Water the third group with a solution of 1 part vinegar and 4 parts water.

    e. Water the fourth group with a solution of 1 part vinegar and 10 parts water.

    f. Water each group with an identical amount of water each day. Be sure that all of the plants are exposed to the same amounts of light and heat.

    g. In a journal write how much you water the plants each day and whether you turn the containers to be sure that all the plants receive equal amounts of heat and light. Sketch the plants every day to show their growth. Hypothesize what will happen to plants in each group. Do the results support or disprove your hypothesis?

Fig. 5.2. Effect of Acid Rain on Growing Plants.

7. When acid rain collects in bodies of water, it threatens plant and animal life. Take two large, identical jars. Fill the first jar three-quarters full of water. Fill the second one three-quarters full of white vinegar. In each jar place leaves, chicken bones, a boiled egg with the shell on, scraps of newspaper, seashells, and other bits of trash or food. Observe and compare the contents of the jars over the course of several days. What conclusions can you make?

8. Because lakes are formed over various kinds of bedrock, they react differently to acid rain. Some types of bedrock can neutralize acid. For example, limestone bedrock can neutralize acid, but granite bedrock cannot. Acid rain is more harmful to lakes with bedrock that cannot neutralize acid. You can simulate the effects of different kinds of bedrock on acidity.

a. Fill two jars with white vinegar.

b. Put a piece of granite in one jar and a piece of limestone in the other.

c. Test the pH of the water once a day or once a week. Note the pH of each jar on a chart. What happened to the pH in each jar? Which type of rock would be best for constructing buildings or monuments? For more information read "Rain, Rain Go Away," by Michael Dispezio, in *Science Scope* (volume 15, number 1, September 1991).

9. In the library media center, research the bedrock formations of North America and Europe. Use geological maps in atlases or encyclopedias. Places with little or no limestone are particularly sensitive to acid rain. This includes a large area of Canada called the Canadian Shield and much of the Scandinavian Peninsula.

10. Many areas of North America, such as Ontario, were once under glaciers. In some relatively flat areas with poor drainage, the ground remained wet and spongy after the glaciers retreated. This type of wetland is called a bog. On topographical maps bogs are indicated with a symbol defined in the legend or key. Using topographical maps, find bogs near Lake Windigo or in your state.

11. Peat moss is the dried remains of sphagnum moss, which grows in low-lying, wet regions.

a. Inspect peat moss using a hand lens. If possible, compare peat moss with a live sphagnum plant.

b. Determine how much water peat moss will hold. Place some peat moss in a kitchen strainer or funnel lined with a coffee filter. Slowly pour water, 1 cup at a time, onto the peat until it is saturated. Leave the peat moss in the strainer for several days. Record how much water is needed to saturate the peat moss and how moist the peat moss is after several days.

c. Repeat the experiment with several types of soil, including sand and potting soil. Compare the results. Which material holds the most water for the longest period of time? Which soils remained moist? Which dried out? What does this tell you about the best soil for growing plants?

d. Allow some peat moss to sit in water for several days. Notice the color of the water. Measure its pH. Is a bog likely to be acidic or basic? Why?

12. *The Incredible Journey* takes place in a forested area of western Ontario. Select a small forested area near your school for a detailed investigation of tree species. You will use a technique called a transect for sampling the number of trees along a line through the woods. For a class of 20 you will need a piece of rope 100 feet long.

a. With your classmates, stretch the rope out through the woods. Try to keep the rope as straight as possible. Your teacher will assign each student a place to stand along the rope. You will be five feet from your neighbor on either side, and you will all face the same direction. Count how many trees of each species you see between you and the student in front of you. *The Golden Nature Guide to Trees* (New York: Golden Press) is a good resource for this activity.

b. Note the nature of the soil and the features of the forest floor in your area.

c. Count how many trees of each species are in your area. Does one species dominate? Is one species found only in a certain area or on the edge of the woods?

d. Sketch a map of the area around your transect. Combine the map with classmates' maps to form a large map of the entire area. Display the composite map with a list of the major findings of the class.

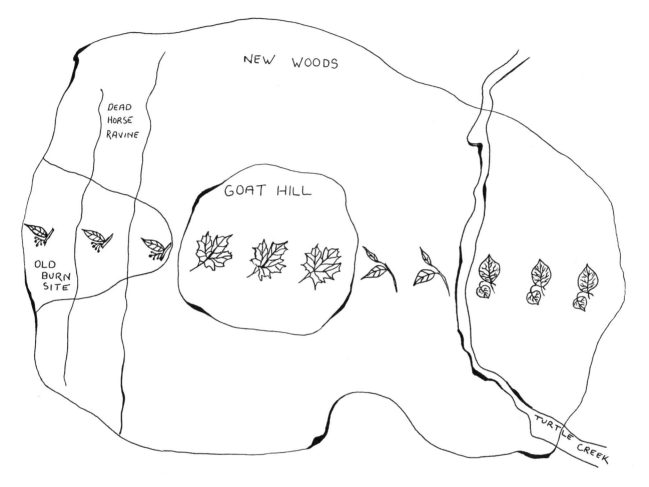

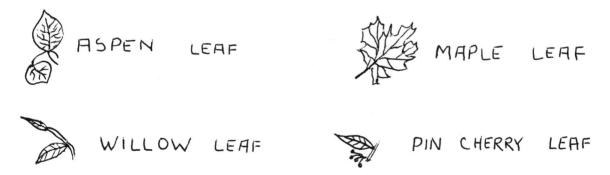

Fig. 5.3. Forest Transect-Tree Inventory.

13. Obtain several recently cut logs. If possible, use logs from trees that grew in your area. Have an adult saw across the logs to cut off several slices or disks. Sand the disks lightly with sand paper if they are rough. The disks show the tree rings, which record the age of the tree and the weather conditions of the summers during which the tree grew. If you can't make your own disks, you can buy them from a laboratory supply house like Delta Education, P.O. Box 3000, Nashua, NH 03061-3000.

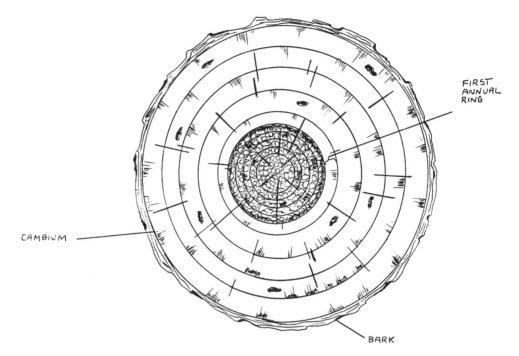

Fig. 5.4. Tree Cross Sections.

a. Count the rings from the center to the outside edge of the disk. If a tree produces one growth ring each year, how old was this tree? Do all the disks from the same log indicate the same age?

b. Use a hand lens to study the rings. Look very closely for details. A wider growth ring indicates more growth and probably a warm, wet growing season. A narrower ring indicates less growth, perhaps less water or less favorable temperature or both. What growing conditions prevailed during this tree's life?

c. You might occasionally see a trace of charred wood in a ring. This indicates fire.

d. If you can find out what year the log was cut, you can correlate the events in the tree's life, as indicated by the rings, with events in your life. Consult the local weather bureau, radio stations, and library media center for sources of information. Check your library's collection of local newspapers to find information about events that may have affected the tree, such as a fire or drought.

e. Display one of the disks. Using colored pins with little paper labels, mark the growth rings that correlate with birth dates of class members, the teacher, and the founding of your school. If there is enough room on the disk, mark important dates in the history of your community or the United States.

f. If you can find a stump from a recently cut tree, compare the growth rings on the disks to the rings on the stump. The same growth-ring patterns frequently appear in trees of widely varying species. If the stump is quite thick, make a rubbing of it. Study its growth rings as you studied the disks.

14. Using *The Golden Nature Guide to Trees* (New York: Golden Press) or a local or state tree identification guide, do a census of trees on the school property or in a nearby park.

    a. Make a map of the study site using a large sheet of flip- chart graph paper with 1-inch squares.

    b. Divide the site into segments.

    c. Work in groups of two to four students. Each group will take one segment of the area to be surveyed. Record data on sheets of plain paper.

    d. With your group draw a map of your area. Indicate the location, approximate height, and common name of each tree. If possible, collect one leaf from each tree.

    e. After 10-15 minutes, rejoin your classmates and put your data onto the class map.

    f. Count the number of trees of each species. Display the figures in a bar graph. Do certain species grow only in certain niches or locations of the study site?

15. According to folk knowledge, lichen grows more abundantly on the north side of trees. Many stories tell of lost travelers who find their way using lichen to locate north. To test this folk knowledge, find a place where there is significant lichen growth.

    a. Tape a piece of waxed paper around a tree trunk at eye level.

    b. Use a compass to determine north, and mark the north side of the tree *N* . Then mark the south side of the tree *S* . Mark east and west with a line that runs from the top to the bottom of the waxed paper. You have divided the area you are studying into two halves, a north half and a south half.

    c. With the marker outline each clump of lichen.

    d. Remove the waxed paper. Count the number of clumps of lichen that grew on the north half of the tree, then count the number of clumps of lichen that grew on the south half of the tree.

    e. Add all students' numbers for the north side, then add all students' numbers for the south side. Compare the totals. Did more lichens grow on the north side?

    f. Write a report of the experiment for the school newspaper.

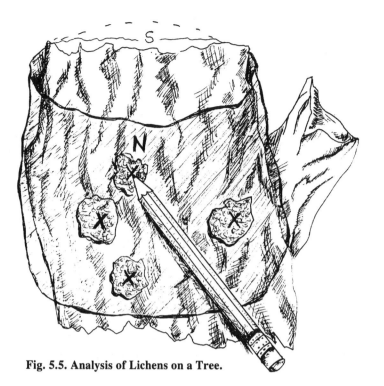

Fig. 5.5. Analysis of Lichens on a Tree.

16. Foresters cruise the forest looking for trees that are ready to harvest. To determine how much wood a tree will yield, measure the height and diameter of the tree. A mature tree is too tall to measure directly; a clinometer and mathematics will be needed. Work in groups of two or three to measure trees.

a. Sight along a clinometer to the top of the tree, and slowly back up until the clinometer reads 45 degrees.

b. Measure the distance from where the person with the clinometer is standing to the tree.

c. Measure the distance from the observer's head to the ground. Also measure the diameter of the tree at breast height (DBH) by wrapping a string around the tree. Measure the string and divide it by π (pi) or $^{22}/_{7}$ to determine the diameter.

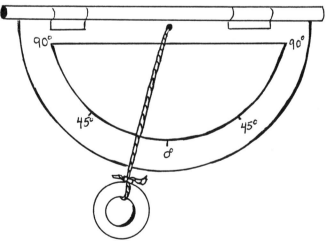

Fig. 5.6A. Clinometer.

d. Add the distances found in steps b and c to determine the height of the tree.

e. Foresters use multiples of 16 feet to estimate wood volume in board-feet. One board-foot equals a piece of wood that measures 1 foot by 1 foot by 1 inch. Use information from figure 5.7 to estimate the volume of wood in the tree.

For additional information see "A Cruise through the Forest," by Bruce Smith, in *Science Scope* (volume 14, number 7, April 1991).

Fig. 5.6B.

NUMBER OF 16 FT LENGTHS

DBH	1	1.5	2	2.5	3	3.5	4
14	73	98	123	143	163	175	187
16	76	102	129	150	173	188	204
18	77	104	132	155	178	195	212
20	78	107	136	159	184	202	220
22	80	110	139	164	198	209	228
24	80	110	140	166	193	211	230
26	81	112	143	170	197	217	120

Fig. 5.7. Tree Volume-Board Feet. (DBH [diameter at breast height] is given in inches.)

17. Ontario is an important mineral producer. Using information from the library media center, make maps, charts, or graphs that depict the location and abundance of Ontario's important mineral resources, such as molybdenum, iron ore, gypsum, coal, oil, and rock salt. Compare the mineral resources of Ontario to the mineral resources of your state or region.

18. Working in small groups, reenact your favorite scene in *The Incredible Journey*. Use puppets made from paper bags or socks. (See fig. 5.8, pp. 56-58.)

Fig. 5.8A. Paper Bag Puppets.

Fig. 5.8B.

Fig. 5.8C.

19. Assume that the Royal Canadian Mounted Police have been asked to help locate the lost animals. Write a detailed description of each animal to help the police in the search. You may include sketches.

20. Write a newspaper article about the animals' adventure. Be sure to answer the questions Who? When? Where? Why? What? and How? To hold readers' attention, answer as many of these questions as you can in the first paragraph of the article. Write a headline that will capture readers' attention.

21. The animals were befriended by the Reino Nurmi family from Finland. Using detailed maps of western Ontario and Finland, compare the two areas, including landforms, timber products, mining resources, and so forth. Why do you think the Nurmi family came to Canada? Would the lives of the family members be very different in Canada than in Finland?

22. The timber and paper industries are important to western Ontario. You can make recycled paper from any kind of scrap paper.

    a. Tear scrap paper into small strips and place them in a bucket.

    b. Add 2 cups of hot water and 1 ounce of liquid laundry starch.

    c. Mix with an eggbeater to form a thin pulp.

    d. Spread the pulp on a piece of wire screen attached to a frame.

Fig. 5.9. Homemade Paper Dryer.

    e. Allow the excess water to drip off.

    f. Open six or seven sheets of newspaper and stack them. When the pulp begins to dry, place it on the newspaper. Roll it with a rolling pin to squeeze out the rest of the water.

    g. Allow the paper to air dry before using it.

       For more information, read "Once Around the Paper Route," by Shelby J. Barrentine, in *Science and Children* (volume 29, number 1, September 1991).

23. *Homeward Bound: The Incredible Journey,* produced by Walt Disney Studios, is a movie based on this book. Compare the film to the book. Present your findings as a written movie review, in a chart, or in a class discussion. Make an advertisement to promote the version you prefer.

24. To bring the unit to a close, try this word search of animals from *The Incredible Journey.* The answers appear at the end of the book.

WORD SEARCH

FIND THESE ANIMALS FROM THE INCREDIBLE JOURNEY

```
A C D E H O N P F K Y M A L L A R D P
C G O O S E S O O M Z P I C K E R E L
A G G N F Q P R X A R B M H N F D E Y
T I R E M D U C K L E B P I K E D R N
R S J V L V X U J A V X Q P V T E M X
O B E A V E R P R I A C R M W D U O O
U K T R U T T I M B E R W O L F D U G
T V Z A W R Y N P O B H S N X H T S R
C H I C K A D E E R C G E K G F W E S
B L A M C M Z D Y E B N F I H K V I J
```

ANIMALS OF THE FOREST:

CHICKADEE	FOX	PIKE
CHIPMONK	DEER	PORCUPINE
BEAVER	MALLARD	DOG
TROUT	MOUSE	MARTEN
GOOSE	TIMBER WOLF	BEAR
CAT	DUCK	PICKEREL
MOOSE	RAVEN	LYNX

Fig. 5.10. Forest Word Search.

Related Titles

Barrentine, Shelby J. "Once Around the Paper Route." *Science and Children* 29, no. 1 (September 1991): 27-30.

Dispezio, Michael. "Rain, Rain Go Away." *Science Scope* 15, no. 1 (September 1991): 38-39.

Levy, Franklin R. producer. *Homeward Bound: The Incredible Journey*. Burbank, CA: Walt Disney Pictures, 1993.

Smith, Bruce. "A Cruise through the Forest." *Science Scope* 14, no. 7 (April 1991): 12-15.

Zim, Herbert S. *Golden Nature Guide to Trees*. New York: Golden Press, 1987.

Chapter 6
The Rocky Mountains

Lion Hound

Jim Kjelgaard
New York: Bantam Books, 1955

Summary

High mountains, mesas, and canyons provide the setting for *Lion Hound,* a story of life in a sparsely settled area of the Rocky Mountain region. A rampaging mountain lion terrorizes the small town where Johnny Torrington lives. The young boy learns much about man and nature as he takes part in the effort to track and kill the lion. At the time this story is set, bounties were paid for mountain lions.

Earth Concepts

Weather; climate; weathering of the land; mountain geology; landforms; soil and rocks; vertical zonation; forest ecology; movement of the earth, for example, formation of mountains, rivers, and streams; avalanches

Environmental Concepts

Predator and prey relationships, including animal versus humans, animal versus human territorial rights, adaptation, forestry, respect for animals and nature, hunting and tracking animals

General Concepts

Love of animals, animal abuse, justification for hunting, mountain climbing, determination in animals and humans

Activities

[Teacher's note: The Rocky Mountains cover a vast area of the western United States, extending from Montana to New Mexico. Kjelgaard is not specific about the setting of *Lion Hound,* so we selected a location based on clues Kjelgaard provides, such as geological formations and population centers. The area that Kjelgaard seems to indicate is near the Black Canyon of the Gunnison National Monument in western Colorado. The closest towns are Montrose and Gunnison. Although the activities in this section relate best to the Black Canyon area, they can be applied to other areas of the Rocky Mountains as well.]

1. Find distances, directions, elevations, bodies of water, human habitations, roads, and other features on a topographical map. Features are shown in great detail because of the scale of the map.

2. Topographical maps use contour lines to depict elevations. On the Table Mountain map, each contour interval—that is, the space between contour lines—represents a 20-foot change in elevation. The closer the lines the steeper the land. Using figure 6.1 find areas that are steep and level.

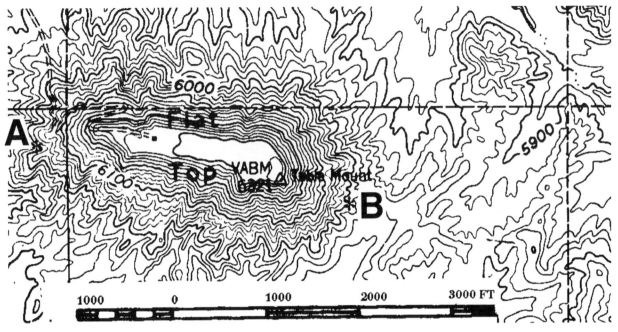

Fig. 6.1. Contour Map of Table Mountain.

3. To practice visualizing map features in three dimensions, convert information from contour lines to a profile of the land. The profile will show how the land rises and falls between two points.

   a. Using the sample section in the diagram (fig. 6.1), have students place an index card so that the edge of the card passes through the points marked A and B. Mark the location of the contour lines between A and B on the index card and record their elevations.

   b. To make the profile, transfer the information from the index card to a graph. On graph paper mark vertical and horizontal axes. The vertical axis is elevation in 100-foot intervals. The horizontal axis is in feet. For each mark on the index card, plot a dot on the graph. Draw a smooth curve to connect the dots. The graph shows a cross section of the geologic features between points A and B.

   c. Make a profile based on a topographical map for the area of your school. Use the profile to show landforms that you can see from your classroom or school yard. Compare the profiles of the land's topography.

4. You can make a three-dimensional model of a landform using a topographical map that has been enlarged several times using a photocopy machine. This has been done in figure 6.2 for Table Mountain, Colorado. The contour interval is 100 feet, that is, the space between each line indicates a rise of 100 feet.

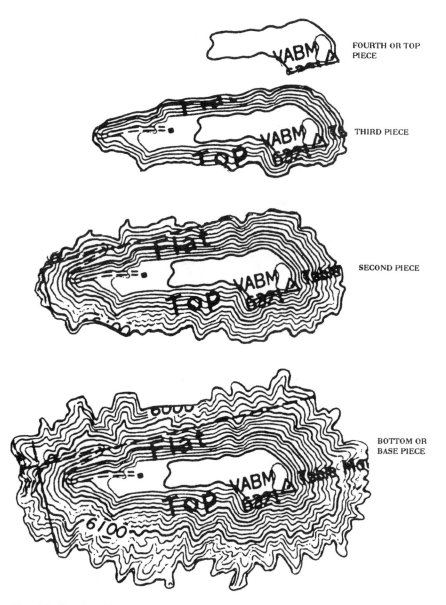

Fig. 6.2. Cut Out Pieces for Assembly of Table Mountain.

Make a copy of figure 6.2 for each cooperative group of students. Using the copies, cut out patterns, one along each contour line. You should end up with a stack of patterns that corresponds to the shape and elevation of the landform. Using the patterns cut the shapes from cardboard, oak tag, balsa wood, thin styrofoam, or another sturdy material. Stack these sturdy pieces in the same order they appear on the map to make a model of Table Mountain as in figure 6.3.

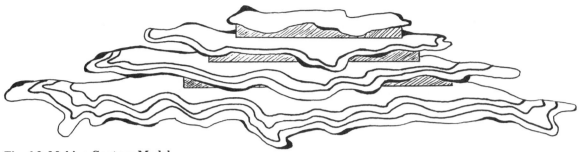

Fig. 6.3. Making Contour Model.

5. Geologists investigate rock layers to produce geologic maps. These maps use color codes to show layers of rock and their composition and thickness. Cross sections provide information about how landforms were created. Figure 6.4 is a cross section of the rock layers in one area of the Black Canyon. The canyon itself is depicted in the middle of the cross section.

    a. On copies of the cross section color code rock layers.

    b. Hypothesize how the rock layers became twisted and folded.

    c. Compare your findings to a second cross section located some distance from the first. Do the same layers exist? Are they bent? How are the two samples alike? How are they different? What can you infer from this?

    Note: A complete set of geologic maps for the Black Canyon of the Gunnison is published by the U.S. Geological Survey (see Resources).

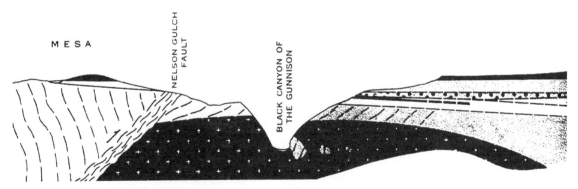

Fig. 6.4. Cross Section of Rock Layers.

6. Mountains are formed by the heaving and folding of layers of rocks. You can simulate this action with layers of colored modeling clay.

    a. Make several rectangular bars of modeling clay; each bar should measure about one-quarter inch. Stack the layers. Gently press inwards on both ends of the pile. As you press, the clay will fold and rise, behaving much like layers of rock. This is how many landforms are created.

    b. Stop pressing on the clay. Observe the mountain formation you have created. Look for cracks, or fissures, doubled-back layers, and other features of mountainous terrain.

    c. Cut open the mountain you made. Study the cross section. Compare that cross section to Figure 6.4 to infer what happened as the land uplifted and folded.

7. Pretend you are a travel agent who must research a national park or monument in the Rocky Mountain region. Use guidebooks, magazines, directories, and other materials from the library media center, and write to the national park service for information. Working alone or in small groups, promote the park or monument to your classmates in a short oral presentation. Include some visual display (a poster, map, model, or travel brochure) to show the area's prominent landforms, and persuade your classmates to visit. For more information read "National Park Getaways," by H. M. Davies, in *Science Scope* (volume 12, number 5, February 1989).

8. The effect of water erosion can be seen in river valleys that cut through plateaus or mountains. You can simulate water erosion using a sand table or box (see fig. 6.5). Line a large box with a plastic garbage bag, and fill it about half full with sand. Scatter rocks to add a realistic effect. Prop up one end of the box 6–8 inches. At the high end of the box, drizzle water onto the sand. Observe as valleys are formed by water erosion. The deeper the sand, the deeper the erosion. The two buckets need to be the same size and about twice as large as the amount of water added to the erosion box.

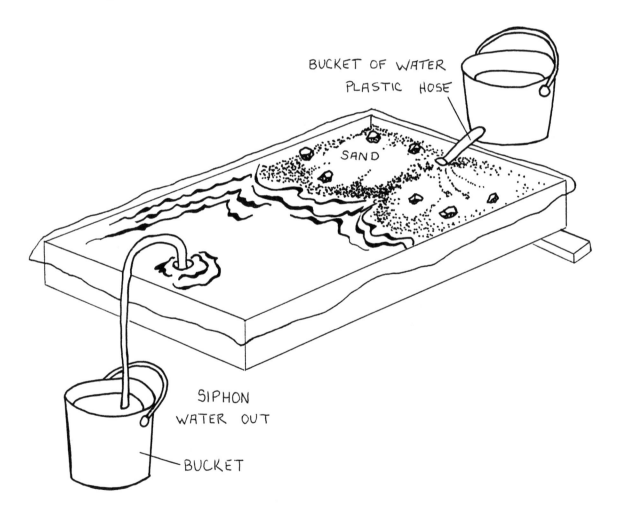

Fig. 6.5. Erosion Activity Box.

9. A stream's flow serves to sort materials. You can simulate this using a 4-foot length of gutter. Cover the bottom of the gutter with a mixture of sand, soil, and pebbles. Place one end of the gutter in a bucket. Prop up the other end 10 inches. Slowly pour water into the top end. Observe what happens to the sand, soil, and pebbles. Redo the experiment, varying the slope of the gutter, the materials in it, and the amount and speed of the water. What happens when the water is poured in gently? What happens when a lot of water is poured in quickly? The latter corresponds to rainstorms or spring runoff, when snow in higher elevations melts and runs down the mountains. How do your observations help you to understand the formation of canyons?

10. The effect of ice on land is called glaciation. You can simulate glaciation. Make a large ice cube by freezing water in a bread pan. Line a large, sturdy, 4-inch deep box with a plastic bag, or use a plastic container. Fill the box with about 2 inches of soil, sand, small rocks, and pebbles. Make hills and valleys for a realistic look. Prop up one end of the box about 8 inches. Place a cake of ice in the dirt at the top end of the box and let it slowly slide. To speed the process, you may move the ice by hand, but be sure to allow it time to melt as you slide it. The melting will increase the glaciation. Observe the glacier's effect on the soil, the movement of materials, and the topography. Allow the ice to rest for 10–15 minutes and move it again. What additional effects do you see? When the ice melts, does it leave a puddle or wet spot? What happened to the water? What does this simulation tell you about the formation of mountains, ridges, rivers and valleys, lakes and ponds, and swamps and bogs?

11. As water freezes it expands, since ice occupies more space than water. If water seeps into crevices in rocks and then freezes, it will expand and break the rock. You can see the force of ice by freezing water in a plastic jar. Fill a plastic jar with water and screw on the lid. Put the jar in a freezer for 2 or 3 days. Observe the results. DO NOT USE A GLASS JAR. It may break.

12. To show the effects of extreme heat and cold on rocks, place marbles in a covered frying pan. Heat the pan on a stove or hot plate for three minutes. Quickly transfer the marbles into a clear, plastic container of ice water and cover. Cracks will appear throughout the marbles; this results from the immense pressure caused by the quick temperature change. In the natural world, quick temperature changes are caused by volcanic action, the heat of the sun, and so forth. This is one means by which rocks break down into pieces and then into soil. For more information read "A Lesson on Rocks and Weathering," by Karen Lind, in *Science and Children* (volume 26, number 8, May 1989).

13. Weathering and the atmosphere change the outward appearance of rock. To see the true color and composition of rock, you must break it open. Put a rock in a heavy cloth bag or wrap it in a towel. Lay it on a firm surface. Put on protective eye gear. Hit the rock through the cloth with a hammer. One sharp blow should break the rock enough to expose the inside. Remove the rock from the bag. Use a hand lens to observe the rock. Wetting the rock enhances the detail. Write a detailed description of what you see.

14. Obtain a detailed state highway map from the library media center or local auto club. On the map locate the Gunnison River basin, the Black Canyon of the Gunnison, Montrose, and Gunnison. Draw a circle that takes in the landforms and cities; the circle should be about 100 miles in diameter. Within that circle find other towns and cities, major highways, secondary roads, airports, railroads, recreational areas, campgrounds, lakes, mines, ski areas, rivers, and streams. What are the elevations of the mountains? What are the

approximate populations of the towns? What conclusions can you make about the geological, geographical, and social conditions in the area?

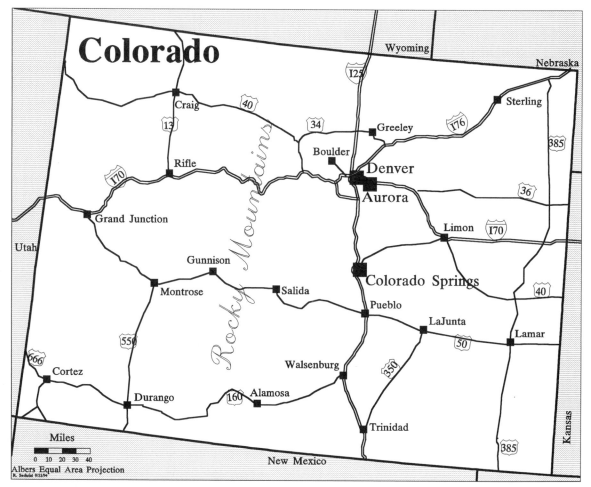

Fig. 6.6. Colorado Place Locator Map.

15. Assume that Johnny lives in Montrose, Colorado. What can you infer about his everyday life from the Colorado highway map? In small groups, discuss one of the following topics.

What landforms would you see if you visited this area?

What would Johnny's life be like at school, at home, with friends, and so forth?

Based on the map, what conclusions can you draw about transportation and travel?

How would the altitude and climate differ from the altitude and climate where you live?

a. After you discuss a topic in your small group, join the class to compare and contrast life in western Colorado with life in your area.

b. Write a story or some journal entries about a typical day in your life as if you were living in Montrose, Colorado. Pick a season of the year to help you be specific about your activities. Assume that you are living in Montrose, not visiting, so you would be attending school.

16. Caves exist in almost every one of the United States. Visit a cave or obtain information about caves in your area. Two good sources of information about caves are state or local tourist bureaus and the school library media center.

    a. Where are the caves in your state?

    b. How were the caves formed?

    c. How and when were the caves discovered?

    d. Describe the interior of a cave.

    Hypothesize what life was like for early peoples who lived in caves. How and why do animals use caves? What part do caves play in stories and literature?

17. Hunting is a topic that arouses strong and varied reactions. Should wild animals be hunted? Does your opinion change depending on whether the animal is hunted for sport or for food? Is hunting helpful or essential to maintaining the balance of nature? Discuss this as a class, then poll other teachers and students.

Fig. 6.7. Mountain Lion.

18. *Lion Hound* was written in 1955, when there were bounties on mountain lions. Public attitude toward mountain lions began to change in the 1960s, and today every state but Texas has laws to protect mountain lions. Discuss why the public's attitude toward wild animals has changed. What influenced the change? Mountain lions are once again threatening populated areas. How might this threat make local residents feel about killing them? Should laws protecting mountain lions be reversed? An excellent source of background

information is "The Secret Life of America's Ghost Cat," by Jim Dutcher, in *National Geographic* (volume 182, number 1, January 1992).

19. Invite a speaker from the state department of wildlife, the fish and game commission, or other state regulatory group. Ask the speaker to describe how the state manages the number of wild animals by establishing hunting seasons and quotas. Which animals may be hunted in your state? Which are protected by law? Do natural events, such as drought, fire, or flood, affect the wildlife census? Are there years when no hunting is allowed? Are there other times when a larger number of game can be taken? To show another aspect of this issue, invite a representative of the local hunting club to speak on the same topic.

20. If *Lion Hound* were written today, the ending might be quite different. Write a different ending or, if you prefer the original ending, justify it in light of present attitudes about protecting wild animals.

21. The forested areas described in *Lion Hound* are populated by cedar, spruce, and pine. These trees help to control erosion on steep mountainsides. Look for hills or sloping areas near your home or school. What types of vegetation do you find? Is it natural vegetation, or was it planted? What seems to be the most effective way to stop or control erosion? How would you describe areas that have suffered erosion? What will be the ultimate results?

22. Obtain a catalog from a nursery or garden supply store. Find pictures of trees and plants that help control erosion. Select an area that is threatened by water or wind erosion. Identify plants that help to stop erosion; consider how easily and quickly the plants grow as well as their cost. Solicit funds from a parents' group or stage a fund-raiser to raise money to buy the plants. Once purchased, plant them and care for them until they can survive on their own.

23. All other things being equal, temperatures drop 3 degrees Fahrenheit for each 1,000-foot increase in elevation. If it is 57 degrees at 4,000 feet, the temperature is 54 degrees at 5,000 feet. Solve the following problems, then write word problems for other students to solve. Use the detailed highway map of Colorado to get the information you need for this activity.

    a. San Luis Peak, about 30 miles south of Gunnison, has an elevation of 14,000 feet. If it is 40 degrees at the peak, what is the temperature in Gunnison, which has an elevation of 7,500 feet?

    b. It is 70 degrees in Gunnison. What is the temperature at the top of San Luis Peak?

    c. If it is 20 degrees at the top of Snowmass Peak, near Snowmass Village, what is the temperature at the top of Sopris Peak? (Map hint: Sopris Peak is northwest of Snowmass Peak.)

    d. There are three mountain-climbing parties on Mt. Baldy (13,000 feet). The first group is at 6,000 feet; the second group is at 10,000 feet, where it is 50 degrees; and the third group is at 11,000 feet. What is the temperature for the first and third groups?

24. If Johnny were to travel to Vail, Colorado, he might take highways 50 East, 285 North and 24 North. Name at least five peaks that measure at least 14,000 feet along this route. List them from lowest to highest elevation.

25. Denver is sometimes called the Mile High City. How much higher than Denver is the summit of Pike's Peak? Pike's Peak is about 65 miles south of Denver and 15 miles west of Interstate 25.

26. Use the wind chill factor chart in figure 6.8 to compare actual and apparent temperatures. Fill in the following chart. What do the figures tell you about dressing to go out into the cold?

Actual Air Temperature

	35	30	25	20	15	10	5	0	-5	-10	-15	-20
wind speed (mph)					Apparent Temperature							
5	33	27	21	16	12	7	0	-5	-10	-15	21	-26
10	22	16	10	3	-3	-9	-15	-22	-27	-34	-40	-46
15	16	9	2	-5	-11	-18	-25	-31	-38	-45	-51	-58
20	12	4	-3	-10	-17	-24	-31	-39	-46	-53	-60	-67
25	8	1	-7	-15	-22	-29	-36	-44	-51	-59	-66	-74
30	6	-2	-10	-18	-25	-33	-41	-49	-56	-64	-71	-79
35	4	-4	-12	-20	-27	-35	-43	-52	-58	-67	-74	-82
40	3	-5	-13	-21	-29	-37	-45	-53	-60	-69	-76	-84
45	2	-8	-14	-22	-30	-38	-46	-54	-64	-70	-78	-85

Fig. 6.8. Wind Chill Factor Chart (Actual and Apparent Temperatures in Degrees F.).

a. Find the apparent temperature:

Temperature	Wind Speed	Apparent Temperature
30 degrees	20 mph	_____
10 degrees	15 mph	_____
0 degrees	20 mph	_____
20 degrees	30 mph	_____
25 degrees	45 mph	_____

b. The temperature at 5,000 feet is 35 degrees, and there is a 20-mph wind. A weather station at 8,000 feet records a 40-mph wind. What is the actual temperature and the wind chill factor at the station?

27. Many groups of Native Americans inhabited the Rocky Mountain area, including the Shoshone, Ute, Paiute, and Blackfoot. Other tribes, including the Cheyenne and Arapaho, moved in later. Research a Native American group from the Rocky Mountain region. Use information from the library media center, and present what you learn by telling a legend, describing the tribe's way of life, or making a bulletin board or display of arts and crafts projects.

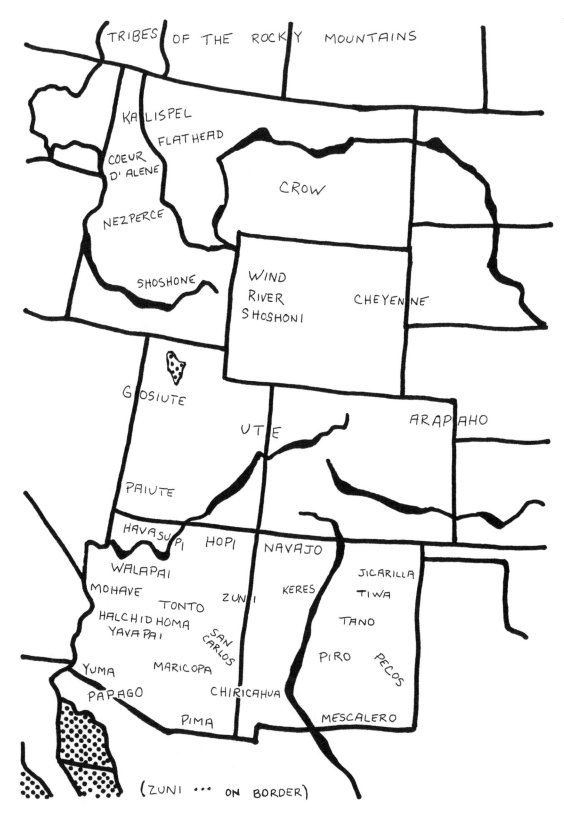

Fig. 6.9. Native Tribes of the Rocky Mountains.

28. An excellent resource book is *The Rocky Mountains,* by Herbert Zim (New York: Golden Press). This Golden Regional Guide describes the history and geology of the American West, flora and fauna, and recreational sites and opportunities throughout the Rocky Mountains.

29. To wrap up your study of *Lion Hound*, try this crossword puzzle (see fig. 6.10, p. 74). The answers are in the back of the book.

Resources

The following materials provide a general guide to geology and specific reference to the Gunnison River area. They can be ordered from Black Canyon of the Gunnison National Monument, 2233 E. Main St., Montrose, CO 81401.

Hansen, Wallace R. *The Black Canyon of the Gunnison* (Tucson: Southwest Parks and Monuments Association of Tucson, Arizona, 1987).

———. Geologic Map of the Black Canyon, Map I-584 (U.S. Geological Survey).

Prather, Thomas. *Geology of the Gunnison Country* (Gunnison, Colo.: B and B Printers, 1982).

Topographical maps are excellent tools for studying landforms. The maps are sold at sporting goods stores, bookstores, or some government agencies. To locate a specific map, you need a map index and catalog for the state in which the area is located. You can obtain catalogs, indexes, and maps from USGS Map Sales, Box 25286, Denver, CO 80225. The name of the topographical map for the Black Canyon area is Red Rock Canyon, Colorado, quadrangle.

If you have little experience with topographical maps, order a teacher information packet or a folder entitled "Topographical Map Symbols" from USGS Earth Science Information Center, 507 National Center, Reston, VA 22092.

Another source of topographical maps is Map Express in Denver, (303) 987-9384. You may order by phone with a credit card.

Rocky Mountain Crossword Puzzle

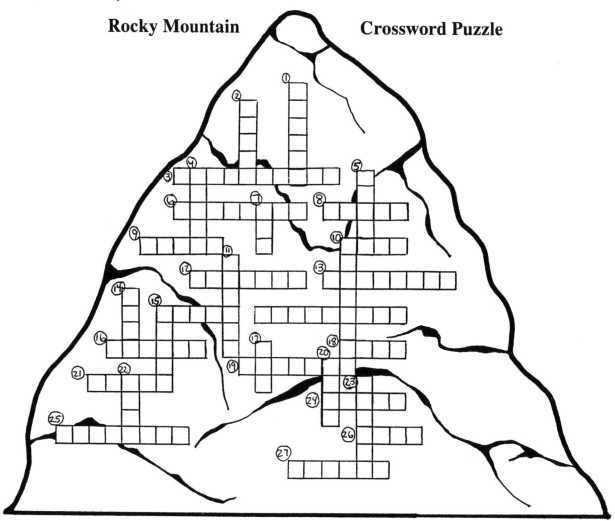

Across

3. A steep slope at the edge of a plateau
6. A rock, pinnacle or column resulting from erosion
8. A steep rock face
9. A natural hollow in the side of a hill
10. The pointed top of a mountain
12. An area of fairly level high ground
13. A swift running animal which resembles a deer
15. The locale for *Lion Hound* (two words)
16. A field of grass
18. A member of the feline family
19. A crack or break in the rock
21. A narrow projection, especially on a cliff
24. A deep opening or gap in the rock
25. A small tree climbing animal with a furry tail
26. A large, heavy mammal with thick fur
27. A North American prairie wolf

Down

1. An evergreen with dense foliage; related to the fir
2. An evergreen characterized by flat needles and sweet smelling wood
4. A stretch of rising or falling ground
5. A pointed structure resembling a cone or pyramid
7. A member of the deer family
11. A deep gorge with a river running through it
14. An evergreen with needles that grow in clusters
15. A line where two upward slopes meet
17. The edge or border of a canyon
20. A hard part of the earth's crust underlying the surface
22. A swift footed animal which has antlers
23. A burrowing animal with long ears and a short furry tail

Fig. 6.10. Rocky Mountain Crossword Puzzle.

Related Titles

Davies, H. M. "National Park Getaways." *Science Scope* 12, no. 5 (February 1989): 16-17.

Dutcher, Jim. "The Secret Life of America's Ghost Cat" *National Geographic* 182, no. 1 (July 1992): 38-65.

Hansen, Wallace R. *The Black Canyon of the Gunnison*. Tucson, AZ: Southwest Parks and Monuments Association of Tucson, AZ, 1987.

_____. *Geologic Map of the Black Canyon, I-584*. Washington, DC: U.S. Geological Survey, 1971.

Lind, Karen. "A Lesson on Rocks and Weathering." *Science and Children* 26, no. 8 (May 1989): 32-33.

Zim, Herbert. *The Rocky Mountains*. New York: Golden Press, 1964.

Chapter 7

Fossils

The Dragon in the Cliff
Sheila Cole
New York: Lothrop, Lee & Shepard, 1991

Summary

Lyme Regis, a small town on the Devon coast of England, was the home of Mary Anning. Mary was born in 1799. To eke out a living for her family, she collected and sold fossils to tourists. Her finds—beginning with a complete ichthyosaur—led to several important discoveries. Although she found the ichthyosaur when she was a young girl, and she continued her search for fossils, she was not recognized for years because of her gender.

Earth Concepts

Paleontology, fossilization, theories of evolution, rock layers (stratigraphy), geologic eras

Environmental Concepts

Land ownership, beach erosion, effect of storms, changing climate

General Concepts

Eighteenth century life, roles of men and women, status of women, class society, education in England, apprentice system, nature of scientific knowledge, comparative anatomy

Activities

1. Figure 7.1 shows the location of Lyme Regis on the south coast of England. Find this small area on a larger map of England.

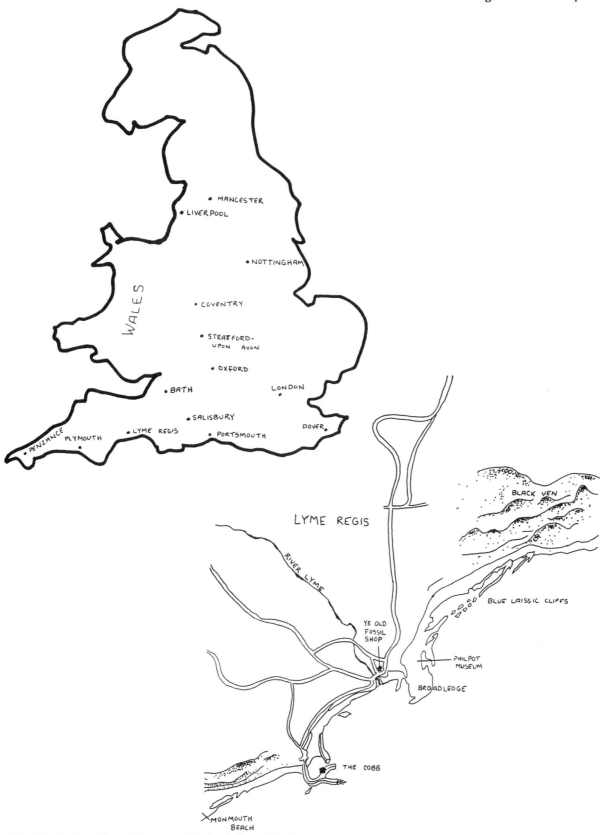

Fig. 7.1. Outline Map of Southern England; Lyme Regis.

2. Fossils are often the impressions of parts of plants or animals. They may be formed during life by a simple impression, like a footprint, or they may be formed after death when impressions of the whole plant or animal are preserved in the earth's crust. When the animal or plant dies, its soft parts may decay, leaving a space that is later filled by minerals. The materials that surround the fossil tell a great deal about the animal or plant (see fig 7.2). If the fossil of a shelled animal is found with sizable pebbles and cobbles, the site of deposition was probably a pebbly beach. If the material surrounding the fossil is sand, the site of deposition may have been a sandy beach. If the surrounding material is mudstone with very fine particles, the site of deposition may have been in quiet water far from shore.

a. Collect some fossils or buy them from a laboratory supply house.

b. Observe the material surrounding the fossil, and describe where you think the fossil was deposited. Describe and illustrate the conditions under which you think this plant or animal lived and died.

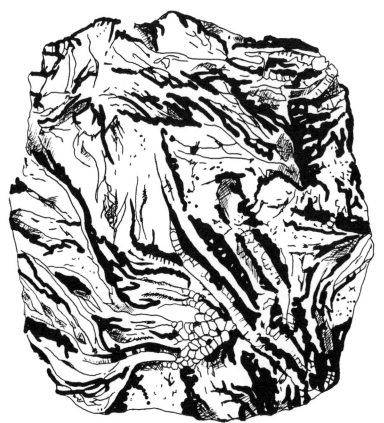

Fig. 7.2. Marine Fossils in Surrounding Rock.

3. To better understand how fossils are produced, make an impression of a sea shell in plaster of paris. You will need

    shallow plastic container or large jar lid

    petroleum jelly

    2 pounds plaster of paris

    1 quart water

a. Combine sifted plaster of paris with cold water. Let it rest 10 minutes to thicken.

b. Coat the inside of the plastic container or jar lid with petroleum jelly.

c. Fill the jar lid half full with plaster of paris.

d. Coat the shell with petroleum jelly.

e. Turn the shell so that the inside of the shell faces up. Place the shell on the plaster of paris and press down.

f. Allow to dry overnight. The next day remove the shell. You have made a mold of the shell. Many fossils are molds.

g. To make a cast fossil, coat your mold with petroleum jelly. Press the mold into the plaster of paris. Allow to dry for a day. Gently separate the cast and the mold. Paint and seal each cast.

h. To make personalized fossils, make casts and molds of other objects, such as statues, buttons, or even other fossils.

Contribute your fossils to a class display.

4. Many paleontologists who uncover skeletons go on to make life-size models of the animals. You can do this using an animal skeleton. The teacher will prepare the skeletons and bring them to class for this activity.

[Teacher: Note: Do not tell students that they are using chicken skeletons for this exercise. The object of this activity is for students to reason comparatively and hypothesize about the appearance of the animal. Most likely, several students will make dinosaurs.

a. Purchase 2 or 3 chickens from a grocery store or market. Use edible chicken to avoid the possibility of contamination. You will need one chicken for each group of students assigned to this project. These can be rotated between groups and reassembled each time.

b. Place the chicken in a mesh bag to keep small bones from being lost during boiling. Place the bag in a pot and cover with water. Boil for about 1 hour. Carefully remove the meat from the bones. If necessary, return the chicken to the pot and boil it until all of the meat comes easily off the bones.

c. Soak the bones overnight in a dilute solution of three parts water to one part chlorine bleach. Rinse the bones and dry them in the sun.]

Students

a. Work in groups to arrange the bones. Base your work on the general principle that all vertebrate animals, such as frogs, rabbits, dinosaurs, and humans, share a basic skeletal structure, with the same kinds of bones in the same general pattern. Figure 7.3, page 80, illustrates the shapes of the bones and their positions.

b. After you have arranged the bones, imagine what the animal might look like. Make a few sketches to help you develop ideas. Select a sketch to serve as a guide for the model.

c. Assemble the skeleton, using modeling clay to hold the joints together.

d. Using clay or papier-mâché build the model suggested by the skeleton.

e. Paint the model and display it with models from other groups.

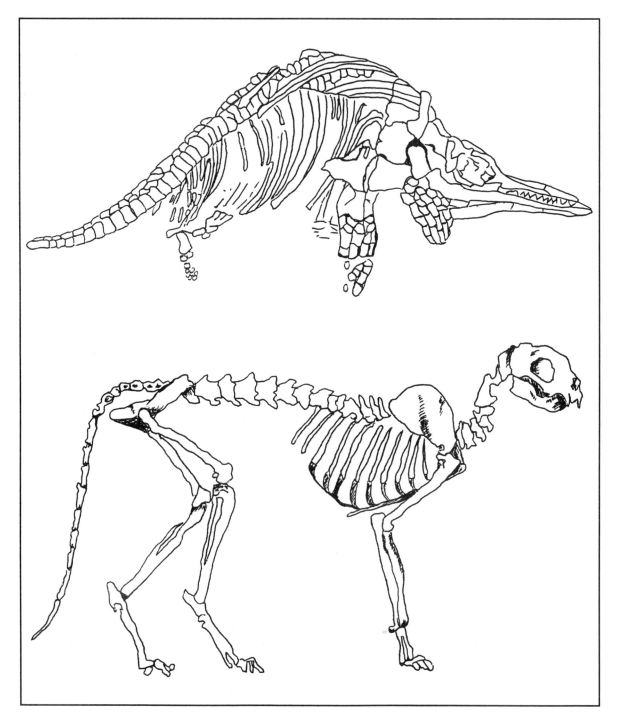

Fig. 7.3. Vertebrate Skeletons: Top—Ichthyosaur; Bottom—Cat.

5. Make a model dinosaur, one that really existed or one that you imagine. If you create an original dinosaur, name it for its characteristics. Use clay, Play Doh, or salt dough to make small creatures; larger creatures can be cut from cardboard boxes, styrofoam packing sheets, or other lightweight material. Ask the library media specialist to loan your class some books about dinosaurs to use as reference.

6. Mary Anning and her father learned how to correlate rock layers by age to help them find fossils from a particular time period. The Annings did this by trial and error, but the procedure they used is quite similar to the procedure used by geologists today. To correlate rock layers by age, you compare rock layers in one place to those in another place. Specific fossils help make the comparison work.

   First, a rock layer is traced along an outcropping as it disappears and reappears in neighboring outcroppings. The layer is identified by color, texture, and composition. Surrounding layers of rock are also identified. Usually, when the layer that is being traced reappears in a nearby outcropping, it is surrounded by layers of the same type of rock that surrounded it in the original outcropping.

   a. Visit a place where the earth has been cut away so that the rock layers are easily seen. (Try to find a cut in a quarry, along an abandoned road, or near a large construction site, where it is safe to observe.) As a class make a diagram of the rock layers. Look for a similar cut in a nearby area and compare the rock layers. In areas where there has been little folding and faulting, the layers will be roughly parallel. In areas where there has been folding and faulting, the rock layers may be more difficult to trace.

   b. If it is not possible to visit an outcropping, use photographs to complete this activity.

7. Periods of geological history are often named after the place where the rock layers from that time period were discovered. For example, the Devonian Era rock layer is named for Devon, England. Any rock layer like the one discovered in Devon, England, is said to be from the Devonian Era. Using a diagram of the geologic eras (fig. 7.4, p. 82), research the origins of their names. Create a bulletin board display, large mural, or mobile that shows one or two important fossils found during each time period.

Geologic Time Scale

EON	ERA	PERIOD	EPOCH	TIME BEFORE PRESENT (IN YEARS)
P H A N E R O Z O I C	C E N O Z O I C	QUATERNARY	HOLOCENE	10,000
			PLEISTOCENE	2,000,000
		TERTIARY	PLIOCENE	5,000,000
			MIOCENE	24,000,000
			OLIGOCENE	37,000,000
			EOCENE-	58,000,000
			PALEOCENE	66,000,000
	M E S O Z O I C	CRETACEOUS		144,000,000
		JURASSIC		208,000,000
		TRIASSIC		245,000,000
	P A L E O Z O I C	PERMIAN		286,000,000
		PENNSYLVANIAN		320,000,000
		MISSISSIPPIAN		360,000,000
		DEVONIAN		408,000,000
		SILURIAN		438,000,000
		ORDOVICIAN		505,000,000
		CAMBRIAN		570,000,000
P R O T E R O Z O I C			P R E C A M B R I A N	2,500,000,000
A R C H E A N				4,600,000,000

Fig. 7.4. Geologic Periods.

8. The ammonites that Mary often found are related to the nautilus shell. Both ammonites and nautilus shells can be purchased in nature stores or shell shops. Compare the structure of the ammonite to the nautilus.

Fig. 7.5. Comparison of Ammonite and Nautilus.

9. The skeletons of some of today's animals differ in minor ways from fossil skeletons of the same animal. Sometimes searchers find fossils of animals that no longer exist. What are some possible explanations for this phenomenon? Use the library media center to find sources that support your conclusions.

10. Check local museums to see whether they have a dinosaur exhibit or a fossil exhibit that may be borrowed. Visit the museum or borrow its exhibit. If there are fossils in your area, collect some and bring them to class or take a class field trip to collect them. Be sure to check property rights and other laws before altering or moving any fossils.

Fig. 7.6. Fossil Shop: Lyme Regis.

11. In some areas of the country, public buildings, such as town halls, or airports, are built of rocks that contain fossils. Work in small groups to find out whether any local buildings contain fossil-bearing rocks. If they do, arrange a field trip to see them. To avoid a wasted trip, it is important to know the kind of fossils you are studying and the source of the building materials.

12. Natural history museums have excellent fossil collections, as do some university or regional museums. If possible, plan a field trip to a museum that has a fossil collection. Your teacher may be able to arrange for you to visit nonpublic areas of the museum where fossil specimens are prepared for exhibition. Talk to the scientists and technicians who prepare the fossils for display. How do they decide, based on the fossil, what the animal looked like? How do they decide how to display the fossil? What do they do when they are working with a skeleton that has missing pieces? How are skeletons held together? How do the scientists identify the type and age of the fossil they are working with?

13. Rock collecting is an interesting hobby.

    a. When you are collecting rocks, record where you find each one. Display a variety of rocks with a map that shows where you found each one.

b. Use a hand lens to inspect the rocks. Create unique classification schemes based on what you see. Some observable properties are color, hardness, luster, and particle size. Consult rock and mineral handbooks for descriptions and illustrations of these properties. Some useful guidebooks are published in the Golden Nature Guide series (New York: Golden Press).

14. Scientists publish their findings in periodicals produced by scientific societies. As a class publish a periodical that contains articles that describe the investigations and activities the class and individual students have done concerning rocks, minerals, and fossils. First establish some guidelines for articles, including

criteria for the reporting of observations;

the form in which the article is to be written, including the length of the article and the style of writing; and

illustrations.

As a class select an editorial board to review articles submitted for publication and to return articles to authors with recommendations for rewriting. Word process or desktop publish the articles selected by the editorial board. Distribute the articles to other students and teachers. Donate copies to the library media center for future reference. Be sure each student has an opportunity to participate as a writer, reviewer, editor, or illustrator.

15. Wind and water had a tremendous effect on the Lyme Regis coastline and its rocks. You can see the effect of wind and water on rock in a cemetery with markers that date to the early nineteenth century. What kind of rocks were used to make the tombstones? What happened to older ones? Is one kind of rock better preserved than others of equal age? Do the older tombstones in certain areas of the cemetery show less weathering than similar tombstones elsewhere in the cemetery? Are there other indications of natural changes on these rocks? Draw conclusions about how and why the tombstones have changed. Can you predict what might happen in the future?

16. Much can be learned from tombstones. If possible, visit a cemetery to look for graves that date to the early nineteenth century. Note information about each person's occupation, relationships, and age of death. Note the number of deaths among infants and children. Do you find cases in which several family members died at about the same time? What does this tell you about life during this time period? Remember the tragedies Mary's family suffered during the early nineteenth century as you reconstruct history from these primary sources.

17. Make a time line based on the span of Mary's life, 1799–1847. On the time line mark events that happened during or just before or after her life. This will help you understand the time in which she lived. Some events that occurred around this time are the presidencies of John Adams and Thomas Jefferson, the War of 1812, the Age of Napoleon, the independence of countries in South America, and the first women's rights convention at Seneca Falls, New York. Look for other events in your social studies book or look up famous people who lived, died, or achieved something special during this time frame. Also look for important events in local history.

18. To visualize the passage of time, unwind a ball of twine, making a knot every 10–12 inches. Each segment of twine represents 10 years. Unwind the twine, making knots as you go, to any year you like. About 20 segments would go back to Mary's birth. Tape or clip cards

at the appropriate places along the twine to show the progression of events. This activity is best done in a large room or on the playground, where there is room to stretch out the twine. Note: Most students in middle school can remember back about 10 years, or one segment.

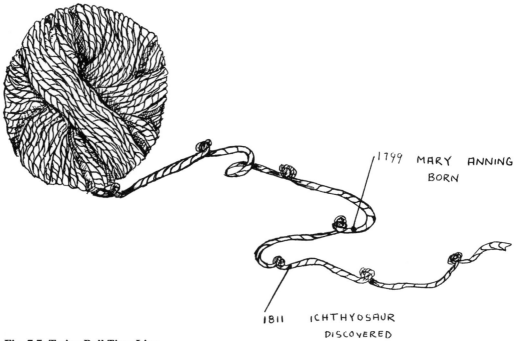

Fig. 7.7. Twine Ball Time Line.

19. Using the dates given in *The Dragon in the Cliff,* fill in the blanks in the following paragraph.

Mary Anning was born in the year _____. In 1810, when she was _____ years old, her father died. The next year, _____, Mary found the monster in the cliff. She was only _____ years old. Twelve years later, in _____, she found the complete skeleton of a plesiosaur. Mary died at the age of _____, in 1847, which was _____ years before the publication of *The Dragon in the Cliff.*

Create other math problems based on the information in *The Dragon in the Cliff,* such as the size of various dinosaurs or distances between discoveries and other places.

20. In the early 1800s there was much discrimination against women, especially in the field of science. Find evidence in *The Dragon in the Cliff* that shows how Mary's work was downgraded because she was female. Do women still face discrimination? Are there laws to protect women from discrimination? Are there areas in which men face discrimination?

21. In the library media center look for books or magazine articles about women in science. Do woman scientists still face the kind of discrimination that Mary did?

22. The educational system in Mary's time was different from ours. Compare the two systems by answering the following questions.

    Who went to school?

    What topics were studied?

    What was the attendance policy?

    What was the apprentice system, and why was it open only to boys?

    What was the prevailing attitude about education for women in nineteenth century England? What is the attitude in twentieth century United States?

    How is education related to social and economic status?

23. How would you feel if you were Mary and had made her discovery? Write several journal entries for the days she devoted to finding and retrieving the monster. Or write about other times in Mary's life: working with her father, visiting the Philpot sisters, exploring with Henry de la Beche. Keep in mind the vast differences between the life of a young girl in the early 1800s and today.

24. Henry de la Beche noted Mary's death to the Geological Society in Great Britain. Knowing what you do of Mary's contribution to science, pretend that you were called upon to speak to that group about her life and accomplishments. Write the eulogy you would give.

25. "Hark! I Felt a Phelt a Knudge!" is a story about a fictional extinct animal, the pointy footed knudge. For comic effect, pronounce the silent *k*'s as you read the story aloud. Discuss the story as a class, then work in groups to write the story of your favorite real or imaginary creature. Describe the animal's characteristics and tell how it adapted to its environment, then tell about events that led to its extinction or adaptation and survival.

Hark! I Felt a Phelt a Knudge!

Once, in the mystic land of Pheltney, there lived herds of happy animals known as knudges. Knudges were peaceful critters with furry bodies perched on tall, thin hind legs with pointy feet. They had long knecks and thin knoses. Knudges used to wander slow and lazy about Pheltney, stopping here and there to knibble knightcrawlers, which they poked out of the ground with their long knoses. When danger approached—usually a person with a knet—they dug their pointed feet into the ground and sped away.

One time, through a mutation—an accident of knature—a different kind of knudge was born to normal knudge parents. This knudglet—as babies were called—had webbed toes at the end of its pointed feet. Imagine its parents' embarrassment! The webbed feet didn't bother the knudglet at all, for it could knibble on knightcrawlers as well as its parents could. And, it could run across the solid ground of Pheltney to escape people with knets. In time it had children and those children had webbed feet, too. Its children had children and grandchildren—and on and on—all with webbed feet. After many years all of Pheltney was inhabited by two kinds of knudges.

Then, through the workings of an evil wizard, rain came to Pheltney. The rain turned the plains of Pheltney to soggy mud, as much as a foot deep. When the rains stopped and the knudges came out of their homes, they found that the mud had changed their lives. Knudges with webbed feet could run along the top of the mud, but the knudges with pointy feet sank into the mud up to their knees. It was much harder for the knudges with pointy feet to walk along after knightcrawlers. And, people with knets found it easier to capture the pointy footed knudges for zoos, pets, and Campbell's Cream of Knudge soup. Pretty soon, the only knudges left were the ones with webbed feet. And that's why in the land of Pheltney, you can see lots of mud and web-footed knudges peacefully knibbling their knightcrawlers, but you can't see a single, solitary pointy footed knudge. If you don't believe my story, ask anyone you meet if he or she has ever seen a pointy footed knudge.

26. The Philpot sisters served Mary tea. As an afternoon treat have an English tea. Serve small, open-face cucumber or tomato sandwiches, bread and butter, cakes, and English Breakfast tea or Earl Grey tea.

    a. To make cucumber sandwiches, trim the crusts from slices of bread and cut each slice into four square pieces. Or use a biscuit cutter to cut small rounds from each slice. Butter the bread. Pile on paper-thin slices of cucumber. Decorate with a dollop of mayonnaise.

    b. To make tomato sandwiches, substitute tomatoes for cucumbers in the preceding recipe.

27. When Mary lived, the harpsichord was a common instrument. This forerunner to the piano was found in the homes of the wealthy, and daughters of these families were expected to learn to play. Listen to some harpsichord music and compare its sound to the sounds of modern keyboards. How does harpsichord music differ from what you usually listen to? Ask your music teacher to find recordings of harpsichord music by Bach, Handel, Rameau, Couperin, Purcell, and Scarlatti.

28. One of the most famous outcroppings of dinosaur fossils in the United States is in Dinosaur National Park, in northwest Colorado. Look for information about this natural wonder in the library media center.

29. For another view of the earth and its composition, read Joanna Cole's humorous account of *The Magic School Bus Inside the Earth* (New York: Scholastic Book Service, 1987).

30. For the latest information about dinosaurs, read "Dinosaurs," by Rick Gore, *National Geographic* (volume 183, number 1, January 1993).

Related Titles

Cole, Joanna. *The Magic School Bus Inside the Earth*. New York: Scholastic Book Service, 1987.

Golden Nature Guides. New York: Golden Press.

Gore, Rick. "Dinosaurs." *National Geographic* 183, no. 1 (January 1993): 2-53.

Part II
Over Sea

Chapter **8**

Coral Reefs

The Cay

Theodore Taylor

New York: Avon Books, 1969

Summary

Although *The Cay* begins on the island of Curaçao off the coast of South America, the main setting is a small, unidentified, coral island somewhere in the Caribbean. Phillip, a young American boy, is washed ashore with Timothy, an older African American man, when their boat is torpedoed by the Germans during World War II. Blinded in the incident, Phillip must depend on Timothy and overcome his prejudice against black people. The two must contend with a hostile environment, including the hot, dry, tropical climate and a hurricane.

Earth Concepts

Physical description of islands, tropical waters, coral reefs and pools, hurricanes and tropical storms, geography of the Caribbean, nature of beaches

Environmental Concepts

Use of environment to sustain life, island as a microcosm, food chain, protective adaptation

General Concepts

Friendship, prejudice, blindness and tactile learning, dialect and linguistics, World War II, commercial vessels, oil production

Activities

1. As you read the book, take notes about the layout and natural features of the island and its shoreline. Note where Timothy built the hut in relation to the island's natural features. Working from your notes draw a map of the island. Draw the map to scale, in feet or yards, and mark the locations of natural and man-made features. Working from your map, in small groups or as a class, build a model of the island. Modeling clay, papier-mâché, and plaster of paris make good mediums for this project. Indicate on the model where the events in *The Cay* took place.

2. When it left Curaçao, the SS *Hato* was headed to Miami via the Panama Canal. The ship's port of call at the Panama Canal was Colón. Two days out of Colón the ship was torpedoed. Several days after getting on the life raft Phillip and Timothy come to an island. Using this information and an atlas, a map of the West Indies, or a marine chart, locate an island that could be the island that Timothy and Phillip found. Assume the SS *Hato* sailed at an average speed of 10 nautical miles per hour, 24 hours a day. Note the latitude and longitude where you believe the cay to be, and compare your deduction with other students' deductions. Find the latitude and longitude on a map of the Caribbean.

3. After the shipwreck Phillip and Timothy worked to protect themselves from the sun. The sun was so hot that Phillip could tell what time it was by the feel of the sun on his skin. Why is the sun so effective in warming areas of the earth near the equator? To explore the answer to this question, shine a flashlight on a ball. Do not move the flashlight or the ball. Compare the brightness of the light on various parts of the ball (see fig. 8.1). What does this tell you about tropical areas?

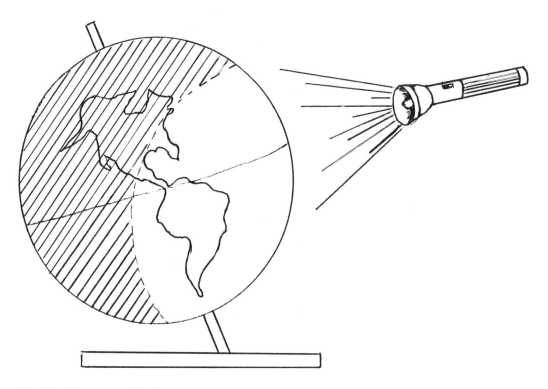

Fig. 8.1. Directness of Sunlight on the Earth.

4. The setting of *The Cay* is a small coral island with poor soil and little vegetation. The surface is limestone with little soil. Scattered about the island are small basins that collect water. How would this environment affect the abundance and variety of life forms? How did Timothy and Phillip use the sparse resources to survive?

5. Coral is the limy skeleton of a colony of small polyp animals. These animals have tubelike skeletons on the outside of their bodies. The tiny animals reach out from their skeletons to feed and withdraw for protection. Obtain coral from a laboratory supply house or a shell shop. Observe the shape of the coral. Use a hand lens to inspect the tiny holes for evidence

that the coral once contained a life form. *Seashores: A Guide to Animals and Plants Along the Beaches* (New York: Simon & Schuster) has a good description of coralline animals.

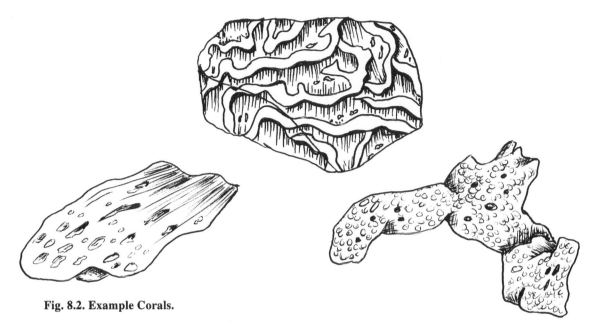

Fig. 8.2. Example Corals.

6. Like all animals, sea creatures must adapt to their environment. One adaptation is camouflage, which protects the creatures from predators. A tide pool may seem void of life, but it is teeming with many camouflaged species. Using shells or pebbles and craft materials, make camouflaged creatures. Create a natural setting that looks like a beach or tidal area to display the creatures.

7. The cay's beach sand was made up of ground shells and coral. Make sand by placing broken sea shells in a cloth bag and crushing them gently with a rolling pin. Using a hand lens compare this sand with other types of sand, for example, commercial sand, sandy soil, or sand from beaches you have visited. Look for differences in grain size, the ability to absorb water, lime content, color, and texture. Note: Wear eye protection while crushing the sea shells.

   a. To compare hardness, make sandpaper. Cover an index card with a thin coat of white glue. Cover the card with sand and allow to dry. Shake off the excess sand. This is sandpaper. Make one piece of sandpaper for each type of sand you have collected. After the sandpaper is dry, use it on various woods and metals. Be sure to apply the same amount of pressure as you use each type of sandpaper. Observe the results.

   b. Measure sand's ability to absorb water by placing equal amounts of sand and water in a measuring cup or graduated cylinder. Determine how much of the water disappears into the sand.

   c. Some sands contain calcium carbonate, or lime. To test for lime, pour a tablespoon of white vinegar on a small sample of sand. If the sand contains lime, the vinegar will fizz. Sands that contain lime are probably made of ground seashells.

8. Many varieties of sea life are described in *The Cay:* langouste (spiny lobsters), mussels, skates, sea urchins, scallops, sharks, pompano, and barracuda. Each is part of the food chain. Research the feeding habits of these animals and construct a food chain for a bulletin board display. Add other sea animals that are native to the Caribbean.

9. A hurricane has a devastating effect on Phillip's ability to survive. Each year hurricanes take many lives and greatly affect the economy of the West Indies. Using magazines and newspapers in the library media center, investigate the effects of a hurricane, for example, Hugo (September 16–22, 1989). Use the almanac to find out when other major hurricanes hit this area. Make bar graphs to compare the severity of these hurricanes.

10. If school is in session when a hurricane develops in some part of the world, watch Weather Channel reports to track the storm's development and path. Plot the path of the hurricane on a map. Using a hurricane plotting chart and data (fig. 8.3), chart the path of Hurricane Harry.

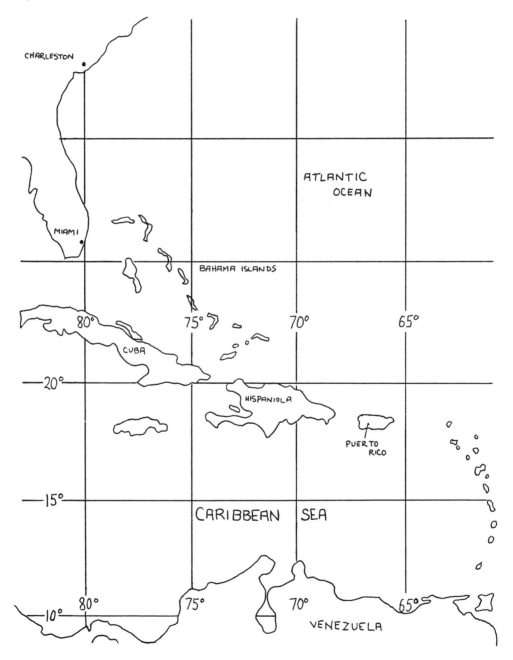

Fig. 8.3A. Hurricane Plotting Chart.

DATE	TIME	LATITUDE	LONGITUDE	WIND (KM)	FLOOD (FT)	RAIN (IN)
9/18	3:23am	17N	64W	120	8	10
9/19	4:55pm	18N	66W	110	6	15
9/19	10:18pm	19N	67W	100	5	10
9/20	3:45am	20N	67W	95	5	10
9/20	3:35pm	24N	70W	90	NA	NA
9/20	3:59pm	25N	71W	90	NA	NA
9/20	10:06pm	27N	73W	90	NA	NA
9/21	3:39am	28N	74W	95	NA	NA
9/21	10:40am	29N	76W	95	10	10
9/21	7:25pm	30N	78W	100	13	10
9/21	9:58pm	31N	78W	120	15	10
9/22	3:42am	32N	80W	60	14	10

NA = data not available

Fig. 8.3B. Data for Hurricane Plotting Chart. Adapted from "Tracking a Hurricane-On the Frontier of Weather Forecasting" Washington, D.C.: National Science Foundation, 1991.

    a. "Hurricane," by Ben Funk, in *National Geographic* (volume 158, number 3, September 1980), discusses the devastation caused by hurricanes Frederick and David in the Caribbean and Gulf of Mexico. Compare the hurricane you tracked with those described and mapped in the article.

11. The American Red Cross provides pamphlets about preparing for hurricanes and other storms. Obtain and read copies of the pamphlets. Discuss what precautions you should take before a storm and what items you would need to survive it.

12. Some islands of the West Indies and Caribbean are the Bahamas, Puerto Rico, Haiti, Martinique, Jamaica, Trinidad, Aruba, Curaçao, St. Croix, and Cuba. Locate these islands on a map of the West Indies. Use resources in the library media center to answer the following questions.

Which European country colonized each island?

Which languages have been or are spoken on each island?

Phillip realizes that both he and Timothy are Americans despite the fact that they were born many miles apart and they speak differently. Why do they speak differently?

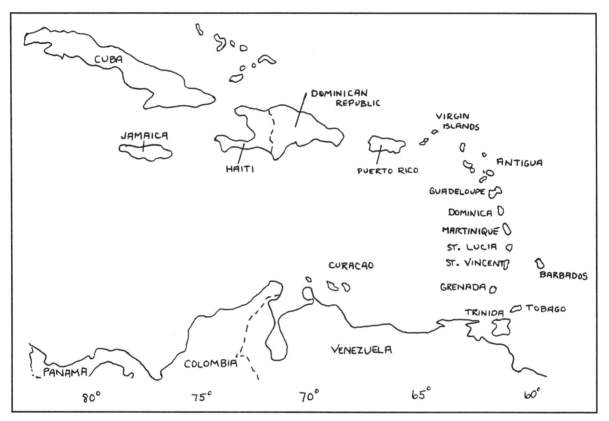

Fig. 8.4. Outline Map of Islands in the Caribbean.

13. Cultural differences among the Caribbean island nations can be seen in the food, clothing, architecture, festivals, religion, music, and dance of the various islands. Have a cultural fiesta in your classroom. Work in small groups to share the major cultures of the West Indies through activities or presentations.

14. Tourism is a major industry in the West Indies and Caribbean Islands. To better grasp the diversity among the islands, work individually or in small groups to produce a travel brochure for a major Caribbean island. Consult maps that show landforms, vegetation, population density, temperature, and other characteristics. Also consult travel books, natural history magazines, encyclopedias, and information from travel agents. The purpose of the brochure is to entice visitors to the island by stressing its natural beauty, climate, historic sites, entertainment, cultural events, and so forth. Compare your brochure to brochures for other islands.

15. Curaçao was an important source of refined oil during World War II. Check an almanac in the library media center to see whether Curaçao still refines oil. Are the other islands of the Netherlands Antilles still involved in this industry?

16. Oil tankers are large, flat-bottom vessels designed to carry as much cargo as possible. Why are tankers built that way? Prove your hypothesis by building boats of various shapes from thin sheets of modeling clay or pieces of aluminum foil. Float each boat in a pan of water and load it with paper clips. Which shape of boat holds the most paper clips before sinking? Use bar graphs to show your discoveries.

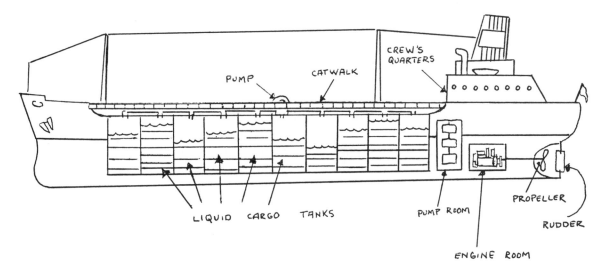

Fig. 8.5. Silhouette of an Oil Tanker.

17. In *The Cay,* coconuts were an important part of the survivors' diet. Coconut is very high in fat and calories. How would that contribute to the dietary needs of the survivors? Watch the teacher prepare a coconut and taste its milk and meat.

    [Teacher: Use a household drill to make at least two holes in the indentations at one end of the coconut. Pour out the coconut milk and serve it to the students. Wrap the coconut in a towel, place it on the floor, and use a hammer to break it open. Chip off the husk. Break up the white coconut meat and serve it to the students. The shell comes off even easier if, after draining the milk, you place it in a 300°F oven for 10-15 minutes.]

18. Make a quick and easy snack by combining equal parts of shredded coconut; raisins; nuts; and other dried fruit, such as apricots, apples, or bananas. Vary the snack by adding pretzels or bite-size cheese crackers.

19. Phillip's blindness was compounded by the difficulty of maneuvering around the unfamiliar island. To help you understand his problem, simulate this situation in the classroom. Divide the class in half. While one group is at recess, the other group rearranges the classroom furniture. The students at recess return blindfolded and try to find their seats. The students who rearranged the furniture can help the blindfolded students by giving them instructions, for example, "Turn left" or "Take another step." Or, each student who will be blindfolded can place a personal item on his or her desk before leaving for recess. After the blindfolded students find their seats, switch roles.

    As a class discuss the problems you encountered. How would you help a visually impaired student find his or her way around the school, for example, how would you tell them how many steps between classrooms, the location of lockers and stairs or hallway bulletin boards, and so forth? How would the daily schedule and instructional procedures need to be altered to accommodate this student?

20. Richard Rodgers wrote a symphonic account of the events at sea during World War II. *Victory at Sea* is a musical representation of actual events that occurred during the war at sea, including the torpedoing of a ship. Compare events in *The Cay* to those depicted in *Victory at Sea.* A recording of *Victory at Sea* is available from RCA Victor Corporation, recording number LM 1779.

21. Many young adult novels are about survival. Compare the adverse conditions and how the main characters survived in *The Cay* to the same elements in *Julie of the Wolves, The Talking Earth, Island of the Blue Dolphins,* and *The Voyage of the Frog.*

22. Look in the school library media center or a regional video store for videos of coral reefs.

23. Use sand to make works of art.

   a. To create a sand painting, you will need heavy stock, such as oak tag or thin cardboard, and white glue that has been thinned half and half with water. Put the glue in a squeeze bottle, and use it to draw a design on the stock. Sprinkle sand or bits of shells on the glue and let dry. Shake off the excess sand. For extra interest, color the glue or the sand.

   b. Make sand paintings on colored glass or plastic balls for Christmas ornaments.

   c. Layer colored sand and small rocks in clear glass jars. For variety, use more than one color of sand in each layer.

24. Theodore Taylor recently published *Timothy of the Cay,* a prequel and sequel to *The Cay.* (San Diego, Calif.: Harcourt Brace, 1993). The newer book provides additional insights into Timothy and Phillip. Before you read *Timothy of the Cay,* make predictions about Timothy's younger days and Phillip's life after their rescue.

Related Titles

Funk, Ben. "Hurricane." *National Geographic* 158, no. 3 (September 1980): 346-367.

Rodgers, Richard. *Victory at Sea.* Camden, NJ: RCA Victor Corp. #LM 1779.

Taylor, Theodore. *Timothy of the Cay.* San Diego, CA: Harcourt Brace, 1993.

Zim, Herbert S. and Lester Ingle. *Seashores: A Guide to Animals and Plants Along the Beaches.* A Golden Nature Guide. New York: Simon & Schuster, 1955.

Chapter 9

Tropical Lagoons

The Black Pearl
Scott O'Dell
New York: Dell, 1967

Summary

Ramon, the son of a pearl merchant, lives in a small village on Mexico's Baja California peninsula. It is a land of mountains, seacoast, lagoons, and gulf waters inhabited by many species of sea animals. Ramon, who learns to dive for pearls against his father's wishes, finds the great Pearl of Heaven. But taking the pearl seems to lead to a series of tragic events. Ramon's decision about the fate of the pearl is made against a backdrop of superstition and religious fervor.

Earth Concepts

Oceanography, marine life, weather and climate, landforms, wind

Environmental Concepts

Resources of the sea, relationship of people to the sea, ownership of marine resources

General Concepts

Cultural diversity, village life in Baja California, the pearl industry, good versus evil, superstition versus rationalism, oral tradition

Activities

1. Using a detailed map of Baja California, like the one found in the *National Geographic Atlas,* decide where this story might have taken place. Skim *The Black Pearl* to find references to landforms, marine features, place names, and the position of the sun. Work in groups to compare the clues in the novel to the information in the atlas. In a class discussion, name the place that your group thinks provides the setting for the story and explain why. Evaluate other groups' choices. Do they match the clues in the book? After the class discussion, take a class vote on where the book is set. After reading the book, check the map again to see how close you came to the location the author described.

2. Studying various types of maps in conjunction can give you a complete picture of a specific geographical region. Study the area around La Paz, Mexico, using maps that show landforms, precipitation, population density, surface temperature, natural and man-made products, and mineral resources. See how many questions you can write about the lives of the people who live in this area. Use the maps to answer your questions. Some questions might be: Is this an area of dense population? Why? How do the people earn a living? What do they eat?

3. A pearl merchant must sometimes travel. Plan an imaginary journey around Mexico. Visit places named in the book: Guaymas, Mazatlán, Guadalajara, Maldonado, Mexico City, La Paz, Pichilinque, and Isla Cerralvo. Research the sights you would see, landforms you would pass, the number of kilometers you would travel, and the modes of transportation you would use. You can make the journey as a modern tourist or as a person from Ramon's village. Use books, tourist guides, a road map from the American Automobile Association (AAA) or a road atlas, and other sources in the library media center. Pay close attention to the key on the road map; it can give you valuable information. One thing the key will tell you is that distance is measured in kilometers in Mexico.

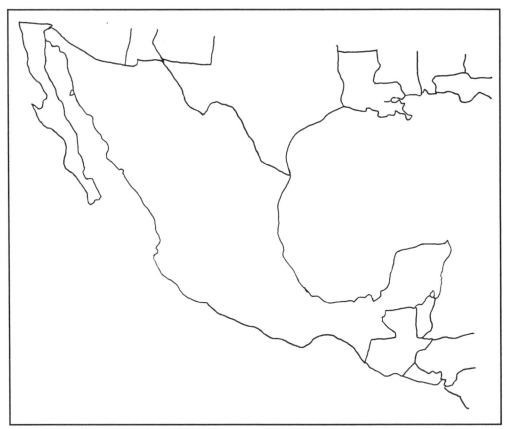

Fig. 9.1. Outline Map of Mexico.

4. From the picture file in the library media center select pictures for a display about various coastal environments. Using what you have learned about landforms and climate in *The Black Pearl,* compare and contrast the scenes pictured. Which picture is most like the setting of *The Black Pearl?* Why do you think so? Why did you eliminate pictures of other coastal scenes?

5. Invite a diving expert to discuss the differences among pearl diving, snorkeling, scuba diving, and deep-water diving. Learn about the pressure that water exerts on the human body, the depths divers can go with various types of equipment, the length of time divers can remain underwater, and what happens when divers surface too quickly. If you are interested in diving, research the topic and report your findings to the class. Find out where you can take diving lessons and the enrollment requirements.

6. The ocean bottom has mountains, valleys, plateaus, and other landforms like the landforms above sea level. You can simulate mapping the ocean floor. Work in small groups on this activity.

   a. Begin with a shoe box and several small boxes or containers. Do not use small boxes made from soft or porous materials that pierce easily, such as styrofoam. Arrange the small boxes on the bottom of the shoe box in random patterns of various heights. Tape them in place.

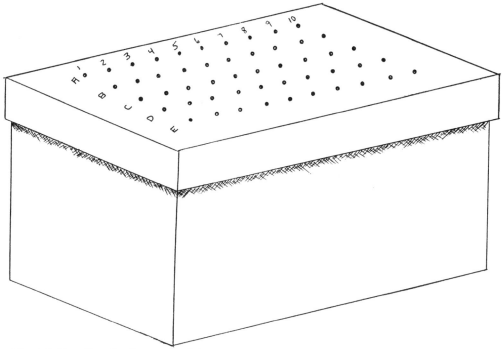

Fig. 9.2. Shoe Box Sea Bottom Activity.

   b. Tape the top of the shoe box securely in place. Tape a grid (see fig. 9.2) on top of the lid of the shoe box. Using a knitting needle or skewer, punch a hole through each dot.

   c. Trade shoe boxes with another group.

   d. Using a knitting needle or wooden kabob skewer, probe the mock ocean floor by inserting the needle or skewer in the holes in the top of the shoe box. Work your way systematically across the grid. When the probe hits something, hold your thumb and forefinger at the spot on the probe and measure the depth from the box lid to the object. This is called a sounding.

   e. Remember that you are measuring the distance from the ocean's surface to the seafloor landform, you are not measuring the height of the landform, as you would on land.

f. Record all the soundings on the mapping chart (fig. 9.3). Make a profile of the ocean floor by charting each row of the chart. (See fig. 9.4.)

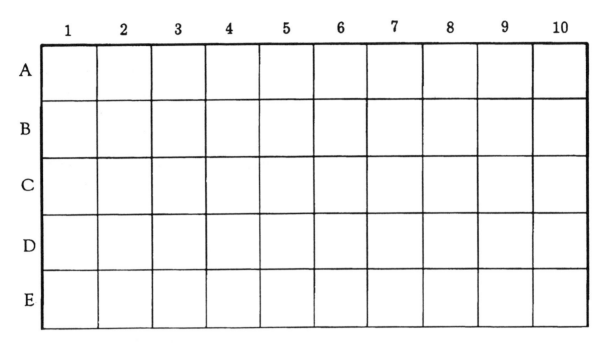

Fig. 9.3. Shoe Box Sea Bottom Mapping Chart.

For more information about mapping the ocean floor, read "The Unseen Bottom," by Marla Stone, in *Science Scope* (volume 14, number 1, January 1991).

7. Bathymetric charts show the varying depths of the ocean much as topographical maps show the height of landforms. Bathymetric charts indicate the ocean's depth in fathoms.

a. Select an area of an ocean, and use a bathymetric chart to find the deepest points in that area. Where are the shallowest points? Can you find patterns that indicate underwater mountains, trenches, or other landforms?

b. Photocopy a 10-inch section of a bathymetric chart. Draw a line across the chart. Plot the depths that the line crosses to make a profile of that section of the ocean floor.

c. Originally, a fathom was the span of a man's outstretched arms from fingertip to fingertip. Why would that have been a convenient unit of measure for sailors? What problems might be caused by using the span of a person's arms as a unit of measure?

d. To make measurements more precise, a fathom was assigned a fixed unit of measure: 1 fathom equals 6 feet. If the depths in a bathymetric chart are given in fathoms, what does this indicate in feet?

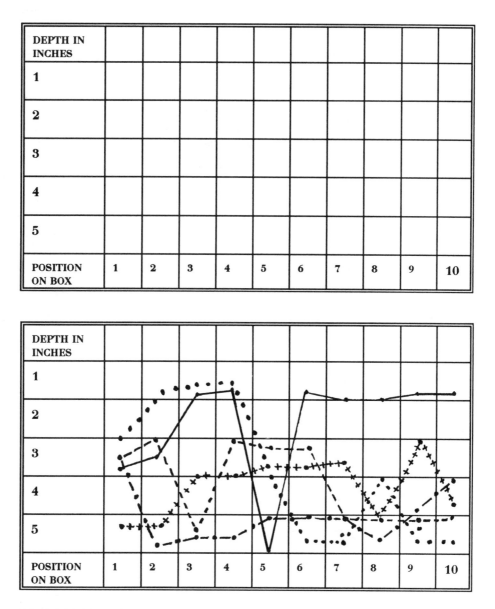

DEPTH IN INCHES										
1										
2										
3										
4										
5										
POSITION ON BOX	1	2	3	4	5	6	7	8	9	10

Fig. 9.4. Making a Sea Bottom Profile.

    e. A bathymetric chart of area around lower Baja California can be obtained from the Defense Mapping Agency Hydrographic Topographic Center in Washington, D.C. Ask for the map titled *Cabo San Lazaro to Cabo San Lucas* (Mexico—West Coast).

8. Oysters, clams, and quahogs are shellfish often available at grocery stores, live and in the shell. Obtain examples of these two shelled or bivalve animals (see fig. 9.5, p. 104). Before class, have the teacher pry open a bivalve for each group of students. Be careful not to use a slicing motion with the knife. Each group should also study a bivalve that has been left intact and compare the two.

    a. Using a hand lens observe the outer and inner surfaces of the bivalve shell. How does the inner shell differ from the outer shell? Why? Notice that, on the outer surface, the shell grows in rings like a tree. What does this mean? Oysters grow in beds on the seafloor. How does this affect their appearance?

b. Observe the body of the bivalve. Notice that the body contains muscles that open and close the shell and siphons that bring in food and release waste. What other features do you observe? How would you describe the bivalve?

c. Compare oysters with clams. How are they similar and different?

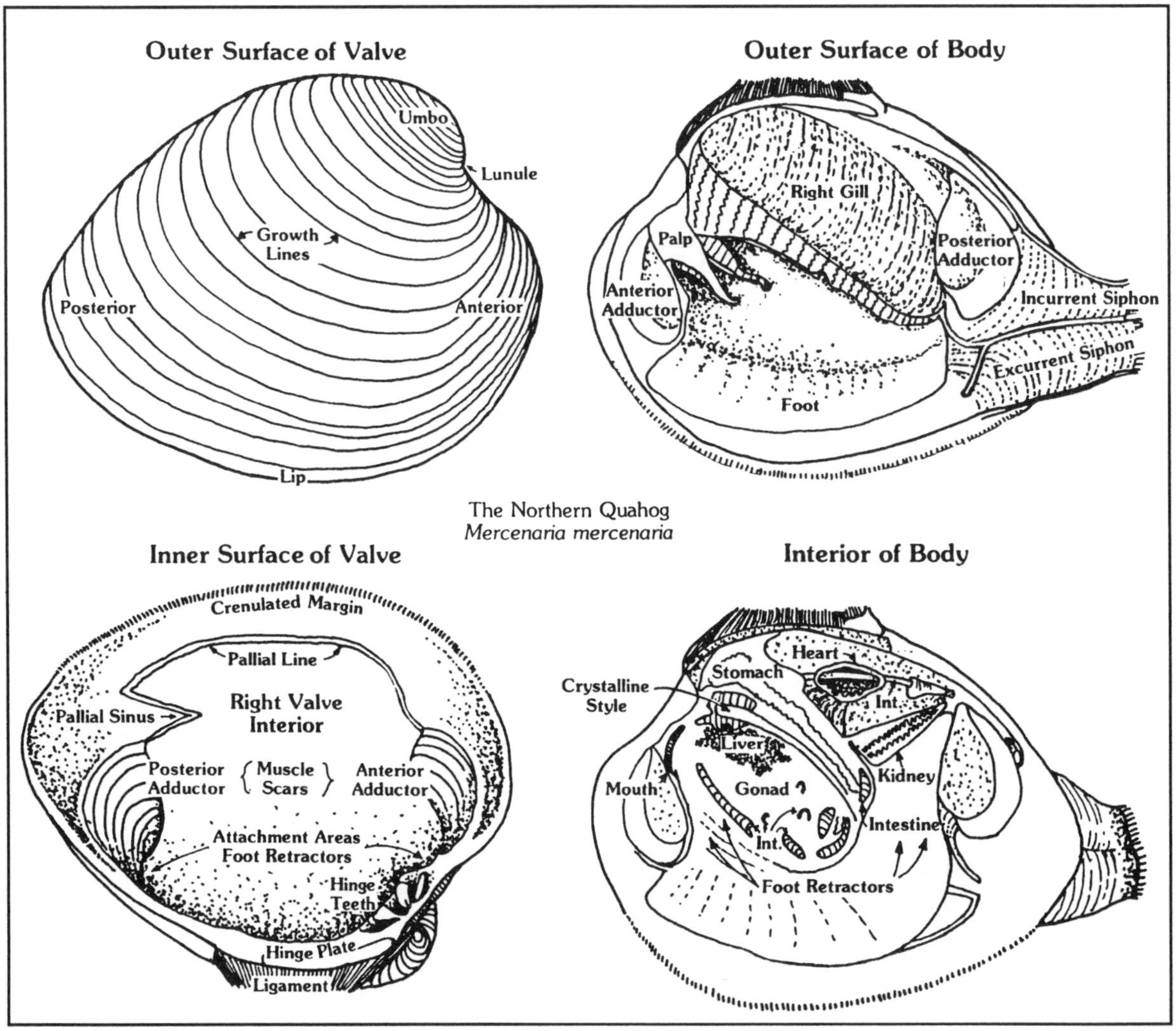

Fig. 9.5. Shellfish Anatomy.

9. The people of the village welcomed the *coromuel* wind but feared the *chubasco* wind. From the descriptions and inferences given in the book draw some conclusions about why. Were their fears justified? In the library media center research other winds and how they affect people, for example, chinook, El Niño, or Santa Ana.

10. In your area are certain winds more welcome than others? Does wind that comes from a certain direction have a specific effect on the weather? For several days watch the Weather Channel or look at the weather map in the local newspaper. From what direction do winds generally come to your area? How do they affect the weather?

a. Use a science or social studies book to find maps that show prevailing wind patterns in the United States and Mexico. What is the general direction of air movement in the United States? Is it the same where Ramon lives?

11. The wind is an excellent subject for poetry and descriptive writing. Write a poem or description of wind or find some poems about wind to use for a choral reading. Ask your library media specialist to help you find suitable books of poetry.

12. Form poetry uses descriptive words and phrases to convey information. A common example of form poetry is the cinquain. The pattern of a cinquain is

Line 1: the topic (a noun)

Line 2: two words of description (adjectives)

Line 3: three descriptive words that show action (participles—action words ending in *ing* or *ed*)

Line 4: a phrase or definition

Line 5: the topic (a synonym for line 1)

Seashell
Rough, oval
Corrugated, varied, hinged
Glistening on the sand
Exoskeleton

13. While the reading *The Black Pearl* keep a journal. Record your response to the story and questions about it. List new words that you need to learn in order to understand the story. Categorize the words under broad headings, such as sea animals, land features, boat terms, fishing and diving equipment, and Spanish language. Examples of categories are

Sea Animals	Land Features	Boat Terms
clam	cave	canoe
shrimp	lagoon	ship
oyster	hill	anchor
manta ray	mountain	rope
shark	precipice	oar
fish	bay	sail
octopus	island	
	channel	
	harbor	

Fishing and Diving Equipment	Spanish Language
knife	fiesta
harpoon	diablo
spear	plaza
sink stone	peso
basket	sombrero
	madonna

a. Vocabulary circles are a good way to review important words or concepts. Make a set of vocabulary cards based on each category above. Write one word on each card. Distribute one card to each student. When the teacher or leader gives a definition of one of the words, the student holding the card with that word answers. For example, when the leader says, "Who is a large roomlike area cut into the land?" the student holding the card with the word cave answers, "I am a cave." Now it is that student's turn to make up a definition to say to the group. The game continues until everyone has had a turn. Some definitions might be

Who is a steep, rocky cliff? (precipice)

Who is a piece of land surrounded by water? (island)

Who is a deep part of the ocean where ships can pass? (channel)

Who is a large, roomlike area cut into the land? (cave)

14. The fate of the black pearl is in question throughout the book. What would you have done with it if you were the main character? Write another ending to the story or indicate why you agree with the author's ending.

15. Many writing topics are suggested by the story. Why did the villagers react as they did to the curse of the *diablo?* How would the local priest react if Ramon had given the pearl as a gift to the Madonna? What would the Sevellino have told his friends in Portugal if he could have spoken to them about the pearl? Write about one of these topics or a topic of your choosing.

16. Ocean depths are measured in fathoms (1 fathom equals 6 feet), and distance across the ocean is expressed in leagues (1 league equals 3 miles). Write math problems using these standards of measurement. For example, How many fathoms high is the classroom door? How many fathoms is the deep end of a swimming pool? How many leagues is it from your town to the nearest large city? What does the book title *Twenty Thousand Leagues under the Sea* mean?

17. The men of Ramon's village are commercial fishermen. In the library media center consult a book about Mexico or encyclopedia to see what products are taken from the coastal waters of Mexico. What is the importance of fishing to the Mexican economy? Compare the size of the fishing industry in Mexico to the size of the fishing industry in the United States. An almanac will help you gather this information.

18. Visit a seafood market or ask the manager to speak to your class. What seafoods are available in your area? From which areas of the world do they come? What guidelines should you follow when buying seafood? What are the general prices of various types of

seafood? In terms of nutrition, how does seafood compare to beef and chicken? Check information on calories, fat, protein, carbohydrates, cholesterol, and sodium. A reference on the nutritional content of foods is *One Meal at a Time,* by Martin Katahn (New York: Warner Books).

19. If you have never tasted an oyster, you might want to try one. The easiest way to do it is to buy canned cocktail oysters. They are small, and you can eat them from a toothpick. Two or three cans will provide enough oysters for the whole class. If you want to taste a larger, fresh oyster you can prepare them fairly easily.

    a. To poach oysters, cook in their shells and simmer in their own juice 3–4 minutes. Oysters will easily come out of their shells after cooking. Drain well. Serve plain or with seafood sauce and oyster crackers. Discard any oysters that do not open.

    b. Scalloped Oysters

    > 1 pint of oysters, drained
    >
    > 2 cups coarse cracker crumbs
    >
    > $\frac{1}{2}$ cup melted butter or margarine
    >
    > $\frac{3}{4}$ cup cream or whole milk
    >
    > $\frac{1}{4}$ teaspoon Worcestershire sauce
    >
    > salt and pepper to taste

Combine cracker crumbs and melted butter. Place $\frac{1}{3}$ of the buttered crumbs in an 8-inch-by-8-inch greased pan. Lay half of the oysters over the mixture. Cover with half of the remaining buttered crumbs. Lay the rest of the oysters on top. Combine cream, Worcestershire sauce, $\frac{1}{4}$ cup of the juice from the oysters, and the salt and pepper. Pour this mixture over the oysters. Top with the remaining buttered crumbs. Bake 35–40 minutes at 350 degrees.

20. Many people, including the men in Ramon's village, earn their living by fishing. A plaster of paris cast of a fish will help you investigate the anatomy of a fish in detail. You will need for each group of students:

a fish (six to 10 inches)	modeling clay
2 pounds plaster of paris	liquid dishwashing soap
1 quart of water	a plastic pail
a shallow box	a cup
a sheet of plastic	a knife
10 pounds of sand	a soft brush
cardboard strips	a wire screen
straight pins	wire to hang something with
cheesecloth	a hammer
a coping saw	shellac

You may wish to do this activity as a teacher led demonstration with students assisting when possible.

a. Add 2 pounds of sifted plaster of paris to 1 quart of water. Stir gently to remove all bubbles.

b. Allow the mixture to sit for ten minutes until it thickens. While the plaster of paris is thickening, prepare the mold.

c. Line a shallow box with plastic. Fill the box half full of clean, wet sand.

d. Make a depression in the sand equal to half the thickness of the fish.

e. Line the depression with two layers of wet cheesecloth.

f. Dry the fish.

g. Place the fish in a natural position, spreading the dorsal and anal fins slightly. Work sand under fins to support them.

h. Pin the fins to hold them flat.

i. Pin the mouth shut.

j. Starting at the tail pour plaster of paris over the fish. Cover the fish so that the shallowest plaster of paris is at least ½-inch thick (see fig. 9.6).

k. Allow it to sit undisturbed 2–3 hours. The plaster is cured when it is completely dry and feels *cool* to the touch.

l. To remove the fish, carefully invert the mold, remove the cheesecloth, and slip a thin knife under the tail.

m. Gently work the tail and body free. Do not touch the inside of the mold. After the mold has dried thoroughly for at least a day, brush the inside with liquid dishwashing soap. Allow the mold to dry and repeat this treatment, which will allow a plaster cast made inside the mold to be removed.

   Make modeling clay dams for placement along the edge of the mold for each of the fins. This will allow plaster fins to be cast a little thicker than the natural fins. Cut small pieces of wire screen to reinforce the fins. Prepare plaster of paris as was done to make the mold. Pour the plaster into the mold making sure that it flows into all parts especially the fins and tail. If hanging loops are desired, they can be bent out of picture hanging wire and pressed into shape after the plaster has hardened slightly. Allow to cure for 6-12 hours.

   Once the cast is hardened, the mold may be broken away by tapping it lightly with a hammer. If some parts of the cast breaks in unmolding, these can be glued back on. The cast can be painted or finished naturally with shellac. A plastic eye from a fabric store notions counter will enhance the appearance of the finished product.

   Note: This same process can be used to preserve impressions of other natural objects, both animals and plants.

n. Find the parts of a fish pictured in figure 9.7, page 110.

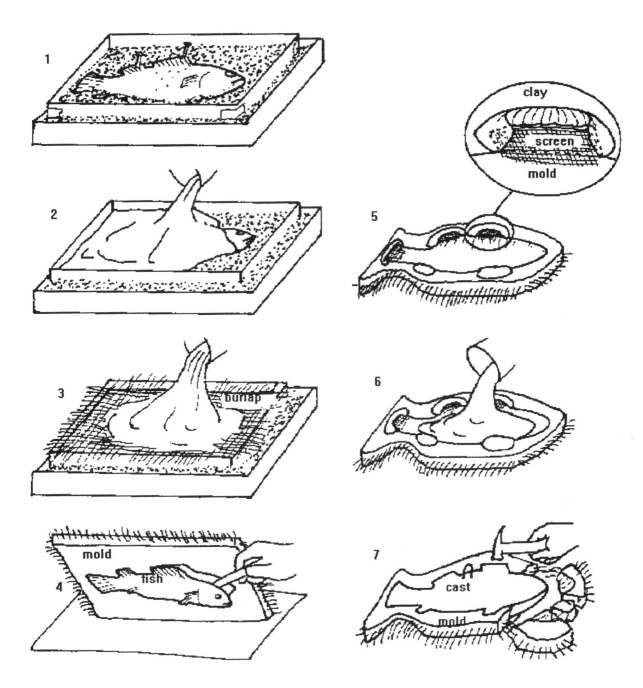

Fig. 9.6. Steps for Plaster Casting of a Fish.

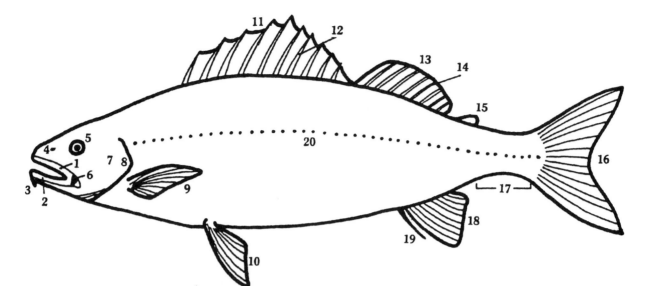

1. Upper jaw	11. Spiny (first) dorsal fin
2. Lower jaw	12. Fin spine
3. Barbel	13. Soft (second) dorsal fin
4. Nostril	14. Fin ray
5. Eye	15. Adipose fin
6. Maxillary barbel	16. Caudal fin
7. Cheek	17. Caudal peduncle
8. Operculum	18. Anal fin
9. Pectoral fin	19. Anal spine
10. Pelvic fin	20. Lateral line

Fig. 9.7. Fish-External Anatomy.

21. Another way to learn about the parts of fish is the Japanese art of fish printing or *gyotaku*. *Gyotaku* is an ancient method of recording fish catches and obtaining information. It is a simple and inexpensive procedure and a good way to gain an appreciation of the form and variety of fish. The procedure can also be used for making prints of other items such as shells, flowers, etc. You will need the following materials:

   rice paper

   modeling clay

   pins

   linoleum block printing ink (water-based)

   small paint brush

   a fish

   a. Clean the fish well with soap and water and dry thoroughly.

   b. Place the fish on a layer of newspaper.

c.   Support fins and tail in a flat, extended position with clay and pin into place.

d.   Paint the exposed side of the fish with ink using a small brush. Spread evenly using a very thin film of paint. Brush against the grain of the scales so ink will build up under them.

e.   Carefully place rice paper over the fish and gently but firmly rub the entire surface of the fish.

f.   Lift the paper off, making sure not to move the fish or smudge the print.

After many practice prints, try printing a fish on a T-shirt. For printing on clothing, use permanent or oil-based ink. Slide several layers of newspaper between the front and back of the shirt and leave them in place until the ink dries. This will keep the ink from bleeding through. (See fig. 9.8, p. 112.)

22.   Invent a creature that can adapt itself to the harsh climate of Baja California or its waters. Begin with a detailed description of a habitat, and then draw the creature, showing the features that make it possible for it to survive. Some creatures and their habitats or characteristics that allow them to survive are:

- an animal that clings to a steep precipice beside the ocean,

- a creature that lives in the shallow waters of a dimly lit cave,

- a fish that lives in sand or mud on the seafloor and can burrow into it,

- a creature that eats clams or other animals that live in shells,

- an animal that lives between rocks or on a reef, and

- an animal that is streamlined to move very quickly.

Write various types of habitats on individual cards and challenge your classmates to create animals that can live in those habitats.

23.   Stories of the devil ray were very real to the villagers. How were the stories passed on? Why did the people believe them? Research other tall tales of the sea or write your own. To learn more about rays, read "Ballet with Stingrays," by David Doubilet, in *National Geographic* (volume 175, number 1, January 1989).

24.   To learn more about pearls and their value, invite a jeweler to speak to your class. Read "Australia's Magnificent Pearls," by David Doubilet, in *National Geographic* (volume 180, number 6, December 1991).

25.   Sailors and fishermen told and retold stories of sea monsters. Write sea monster stories and tell them to your classmates.

26.   Does your class music book contain songs about or from Mexico or Spain? Ask your music teacher to help you find songs about or from these areas.

27.   Have a Fiesta Day. Incorporate various subject areas, such as music and art. Invite parents for a day of songs, dances, food, and appreciation of the Mexican culture. Display pictures and artifacts in a mini-museum to bring alive the culture.

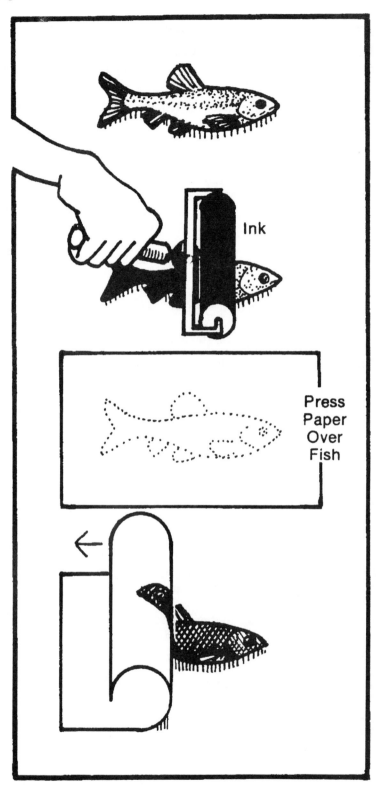

Fig. 9.8. Fish Printing.

28. Invite a visitor to the class to discuss how people migrated from Spain to Mexico and to the United States.

29. Compare the pearl industry of Mexico to that of Spain.

Related Titles

Doubilet, David. "Australia's Magnificent Pearls." *National Geographic* 180, no. 6 (December 1991): 109-123.

———. "Ballet with Stingrays." *National Geographic* 175, no. 1 (January 1989): 84-95.

Katahn, Martin. *One Meal at a Time*. New York: Warner Books, 1993.

Stone, Marla. "The Unseen Bottom." *Science Scope* 14, no. 1 (January 1991): 32-35.

Chapter 10
California Coastal Islands

Island of the Blue Dolphins
Scott O'Dell
New York: Dell, 1984

Summary

When Karana's tribe is relocated from an island off the coast of California, she is inadvertently left behind. Her only companion in the arid environment is a wild dog, which she tames and calls Rontu. Together they must become self-sufficient, heavily dependent on the abundant sea life surrounding the island.

Earth Concepts

Channel Islands and southern California, weather and climate, wind, tides and tidal waves, ocean currents, landforms, caves, earthquakes

Environmental Concepts

Relationships among water, vegetation, and animals; adaptation; food gathering; endangered animals; seaweed or kelp; relocation of Native Americans

General Concepts

Fictionalized historical event, passage of time, survival and self-sufficiency, human and animal relationships, Native American culture, Russian presence in North America

Activities

1. From 1835 to 1853 Karana lived alone in the area of the Channel Islands off the coast of southern California near Santa Barbara. One of the larger islands, San Nicholas, was her home after she left the Island of the Blue Dolphins. On a map of southern California's coast locate San Nicholas, San Miguel, Santa Rosa, Santa Cruz, Anacapa, Santa Catalina, and San Clemente. Compare the islands' locations to San Diego, Los Angeles, and Long Beach. Find a general description of the islands in a travel guide to California, an encyclopedia, or other sources in the library media center.

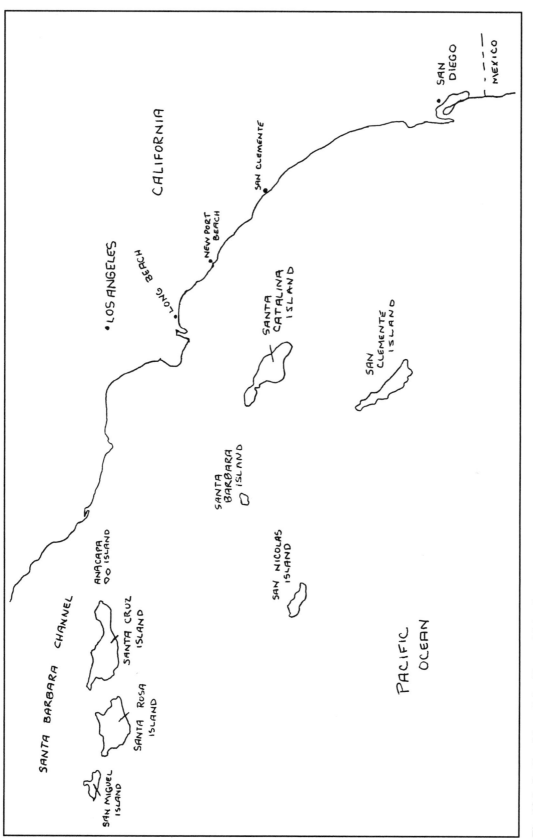

Fig. 10.1. Outline Map of the Channel Islands.

2. The Channel Islands experience little seasonal variation. Still, Karana speaks of the four seasons. What climatic changes occur in winter and summer in the Channel Islands? How are the changes described? Compare and contrast these seasonal variations to the seasons in your region.

3. The earth's crust is not one continuous sheet. It is made up of individual sections, called plates. These plates move. Some parts of California are on plates that are separate from the plate that forms the rest of North America. Scientists believe that as the plates move California eventually will break away from North America. What evidence supports that idea?

    Look at the Plate Boundaries Map (fig. 10.2). Which plates are closest to the United States? What is the relationship between the boundaries of shifting plates and volcanic activity or earthquakes?

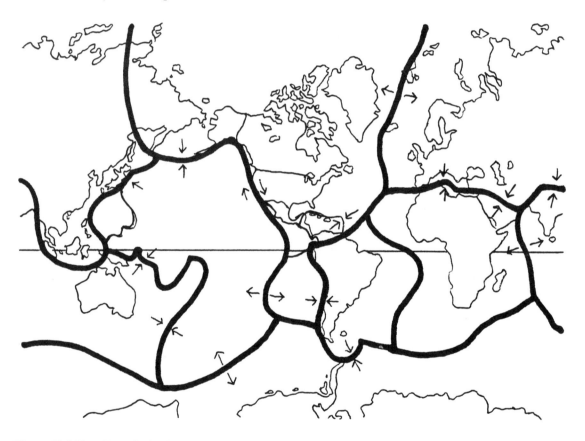

Figure 10.2 Plate Boundaries Map.

4. The transparency master (fig. 10.3) shows three types of plate boundaries:

    lateral, where plates slip and slide past one another;

    convergent, where plates collide; and

    divergent, where plates move apart.

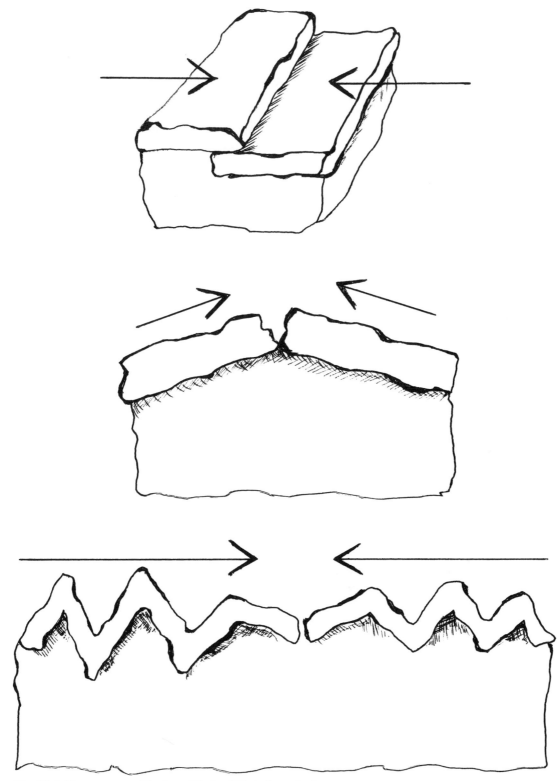

Fig. 10.3. Transparency Master—Kinds of Plate Boundaries.

You can simulate the movements and results with modeling clay (see fig. 10.4).

a. Obtain four colors of modeling clay.

b. Shape the clay into long, flat strips. Make two strips for each color of dough. Make two piles of strips, each pile containing one strip of each color.

c. Set the two piles of clay side by side so that the long edges touch. Slowly drag the piles beside each other in opposite directions. This kind of movement causes earthquakes, and evidence of this type of movement in the past leads scientists to believe that California will one day separate from the rest of North America.

d. Set the two piles of clay beside each other. Slowly move them toward each other so that one layer slips under the other. This movement in the earth's crust produces violent shaking. Separate the two piles and place them beside each other again. Slowly slide the two piles toward each other until they collide. Keep sliding until both push upward. This type of movement also produces violent shaking, and it forms hills or mountains.

e. Place the two piles of clay end to end, so that one end overlaps the other. Slowly drag the two piles of clay in opposite directions. This type of movement could create canyons or troughs.

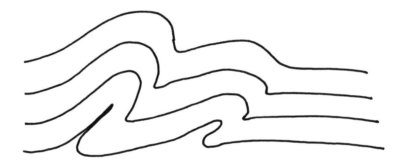

Fig. 10.4. Earth Layer Collisions—A Simulation.

5. Choose a location on the plate boundaries map (fig. 10.2) to research. Some locations are southern California, Iceland, Indonesia, and Tibet. In the library media center find resources that will tell you about the crust conditions in that area. Look for pictures that show evidence of the shifting plates.

6. Working in small groups, cut apart a map of the continents along their boundaries. You should have seven pieces if you include Antarctica and split Europe from Asia. To make the task simplier, you can use the silhouettes in figure 10.5, which only has five pieces. On a work surface arrange the pieces to form one large land mass. Check topographical maps to find similar landforms where the continents touch. This will support the theory that the continents were once joined in the way the group arranged them.

Fig. 10.5. Continent Cutouts.

7. Earth scientists use complex and expensive instruments to measure seismic activity. Simply put, a seismograph comprises a weighted object affixed to a writing instrument suspended above a moving sheet of recording paper. As an earthquake disturbs the earth's surface, waves and jagged lines are recorded on the paper. The larger the waves or jagged marks the more pronounced the earthquake. You can make a model of a seismograph from common materials (see fig. 10.6).

   a. Fill a coffee can half full of sand.

   b. Attach a marking pen, tip down, to the bottom of the coffee can. The tip of the marking pen should just reach the work surface.

   Observe the markings on the cash register tape. To simulate an earthquake, have people walk or run past the seismograph.

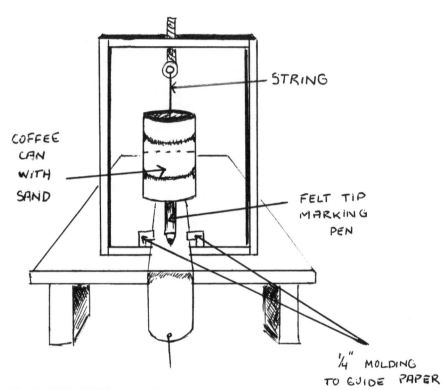

Fig. 10.6. Model Seismograph.

8. Major earthquakes have devastated parts of the United States. Two major earthquakes took place in San Francisco, California. One occurred April 18, 1906, and another occurred October 17, 1989. In the library media center find information about the severity of these earthquakes. Look at photographs of the destruction to see how the earth's shifts caused the land to rise or sink.

9. Use an almanac to learn the names of places hit by major earthquakes in this century. Plot the locations on a world map. Do you see any patterns? Compare the world map on which you plotted the earthquakes to the transparency master (fig. 10.2). What does this tell you about the causes of earthquakes?

10. In a marine environment the effect of the sun's heat on the development of wind is significant. Karana remarked that often the wind died down by midnight but increased again as noon approached. Develop theories to explain this process. Devise ways to test your theories using heat lamps and containers of water (see fig. 10.7)

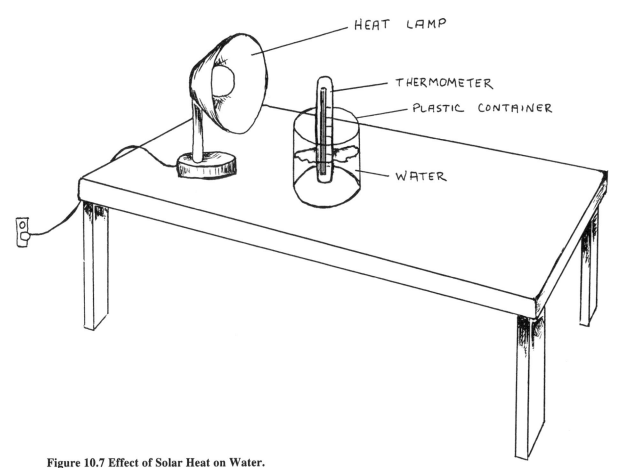

Figure 10.7 Effect of Solar Heat on Water.

11. Someday, the island of San Nicholas may be swept back into the sea by wind and waves. To see the effect of water upon an object, allow water to drip on a bar of soap over a period of hours or days.

   a. Find a container with a side spout. Fill it with water.

   b. Suspend a bar of soap over a bucket. (See fig. 10.8, p. 122.)

   c. Open the spigot of the container just enough to allow a slow drip. Allow the water to drip slowly and steadily for several hours or a few days.

   d. Observe the effect on the soap and examine the water collected in the bucket below.

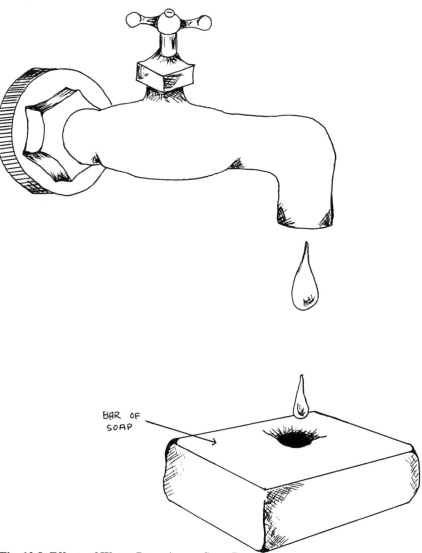

BAR OF
SOAP

Fig. 10.8. Effects of Water Dropping on Soap Bar.

12. The cave on Karana's island was of great value to her. Contact a local or state tourist bureau to find out whether there are caves in your area. Visit the caves or write to the tourist bureau for information about them. How were they formed? How large are they? Are there indications that previous civilizations lived in them? When and how were the caves discovered in recent times? If there are many caves in your state, compare their size and other characteristics. What would it be like to live in a cave or to use one as a temporary shelter? Discuss this from the point of view of someone living today and someone who lived one hundred years ago. How would their points of view be similar? How would they differ?

13. Two famous caves in the United States are Carlsbad Caverns in New Mexico and Mammoth Cave in Kentucky. Research these caves to learn about the formation and existence of caves.

14. Sea caves (often called grottoes) have one seaward opening that is almost or completely submerged at high tide. If the roof of the cave is high enough, the water-filled cave can be a place of intense blue light. Experiment with a round, clear plastic container filled with water and a pinlight source to see how different colors of light are bent by the water. Does this provide a clue to the color of light inside a grotto? Note: Pinlight sources are formed by placing a powerful flashlight or high intensity lamp so that it shines through a hole in an index card in a darkened room. A prism can replace the bottle of water for this experiment.

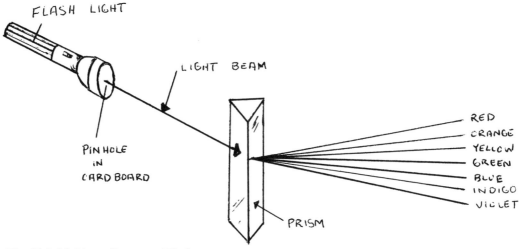

Fig. 10.9. Making a Spectrum Display.

15. The harbor in the *Island of the Blue Dolphins* is called Coral Cove. For activities involving coral see chapter 8.

16. Leagues and fathoms are units of measure for ocean distances and depths. For activities involving leagues and fathoms see chapter 9.

17. Play a bingo game using words from *Island of the Blue Dolphins.*

    a. Make playing cards that have a grid with five columns and five rows. Label the columns People and Places; Sea Life; Plants and Animals; Things in Nature; and Helpful Items. Under each category list five items or places in that category. (See fig. 10.10, pp. 124-27.) Every playing card should be slightly different.

    b. Make playing pieces by cutting a sheet of paper into squares about the size of the squares on the playing cards.

    c. Use slips of heavy paper or card stock to make cards for the caller. Make one caller's card for each different word on the playing cards. Make only one caller's card per word, regardless of how many playing cards bear that word.

    d. Pick a person to be the caller. The caller draws a caller's card from a box and calls out the word on the card. Or, the caller calls out a clue to the word on the card.

    e. When the caller calls out a word or clue, every player checks to see whether the word is on his or her playing card. If the word does appear, the player covers the word with a playing piece. The first player who covers five squares in a straight line wins.

PEOPLE AND PLACES	SEA LIFE	PLANTS AND ANIMALS	THINGS IN NATURE	HELPFUL ITEMS
Rontu	Sea Otter	Cormorant	Cave	Canoe
Coral Cove	Kelp	Cactus	Tides	North Star
Russians	Dolphins	FREE	Wind	Nets
Aleuts	Devil Fish	Pelicans	Earthquake	Whale Bone
Karana	Whale	Roots	Springs	Tools

PEOPLE AND PLACES	SEA LIFE	PLANTS AND ANIMALS	THINGS IN NATURE	HELPFUL ITEMS
Karana	Abalone	Dog	Springs	Basket
San Nicholas	Sea Bass	Cormorant	Cliff	Whale Bone
Aleuts	Sea Otter	FREE	Earthquake	Tools
Rontu	Dolphins	Cactus	Cave	Nets
Coral Cove	Kelp	Gull	Tides	North Star

Fig. 10.10A. Blue Dolphin Bingo Game Cards.

PEOPLE AND PLACES	SEA LIFE	PLANTS AND ANIMALS	THINGS IN NATURE	HELPFUL ITEMS
Aleuts	Dolphins	Gulls	Earthquake	Tools
Karana	Whale	Pelicans	Springs	Basket
San Nicholas	Devil Fish	FREE	Cliff	Whale Bone
Russians	Kelp	Dog	Wind	Canoe
Rontu	Scallops	Yuccas	Cave	Nets

PEOPLE AND PLACES	SEA LIFE	PLANTS AND ANIMALS	THINGS IN NATURE	HELPFUL ITEMS
Russians	Devil Fish	Roots	Wind	Nets
Rontu	Scallops	Dog	Cave	Canoe
Coral Cove	Sea Bass	FREE	Tides	North Star
San Nicholas	Whale	Cormorant	Cliff	Tools
Aleuts	Abalone	Cactus	Earthquake	Basket

Fig. 10.10B. Blue Dolphin Bingo Game Cards.

PEOPLE AND PLACES	SEA LIFE	PLANTS AND ANIMALS	THINGS IN NATURE	HELPFUL ITEMS
Aleuts	Sea Bass	Pelicans	Earthquake	Tools
San Nicholas	Abalone	Roots	Cliff	Whale Bone
Karana	Devil Fish	FREE	Springs	Basket
Rontu	Sea Otter	Cormorant	Cave	Canoe
Russians	Kelp	Cactus	Wind	Nets

PEOPLE AND PLACES	SEA LIFE	PLANTS AND ANIMALS	THINGS IN NATURE	HELPFUL ITEMS
Russians	Kelp	Yuccas	Wind	Nets
Coral Cove	Sea Otter	Dog	Tides	North Star
Rontu	Sea Bass	FREE	Cave	Canoe
Aleuts	Dolphins	Gulls	Earthquake	Basket
San Nicholas	Whale	Pelicans	Cliff	Tools

Fig. 10.10C. Blue Dolphin Bingo Game Cards.

From *Intermediate Science Through Children's Literature*, © 1994. Teacher Ideas Press, P.O. Box 6633, Englewood, CO 80155-6633. 1-800-237-6124.

PEOPLE AND PLACES	SEA LIFE	PLANTS AND ANIMALS	THINGS IN NATURE	HELPFUL ITEMS
San Nicholas	Whale	Cactus	Cliffs	Whale Bone
Karana	Dolphins	Cormorant	Springs	Basket
Aleuts	Kelp	FREE	Earthquake	Tools
Russians	Scallops	Yuccas	Wind	Canoe
Coral Cove	Devil Fish	Roots	Tides	Nets

PEOPLE AND PLACES	SEA LIFE	PLANTS AND ANIMALS	THINGS IN NATURE	HELPFUL ITEMS
Coral Cove	Scallops	Pelicans	Tides	North Star
Rontu	Devil Fish	Gulls	Cave	Canoe
Russians	Whale	FREE	Wind	Nets
San Nicholas	Abalone	Cactus	Cliff	Tools
Karana	Sea Bass	Roots	Springs	Baskets

Fig. 10.10D. Blue Dolphin Bingo Game Cards.

18. Many occurrences in *Island of the Blue Dolphins* would make excellent news articles. If you were a reporter telling the world about Karana's activities, how would you report the relocation of the villagers, her brother's death, the second arrival of the Aleut sailors, the killing of the sea otters, the training of Rontu, her rescue, and other events? Would some events make better feature articles than news articles?

19. You are the pilot of a plane flying over the Pacific Ocean. After developing engine trouble, you see an island and decide to parachute to safety. As you descend you notice that the island is shaped like a dolphin and its center is hilly. After several days of exploring and working on the radio that you had the presence of mind to bring along, you are able to make radio contact with an aircraft carrier. You have no instruments to determine latitude or longitude and must describe the island in complete detail to your rescuers. How would you describe the island?

20. Our society is very aware of the need to preserve the environment. However, we must use natural resources for survival. Discuss how these two concepts can coexist. Do we have the right to use the environment as we wish? Who has the right to limit the use of natural resources? Does the end justify the means?

21. The Russian sea captain ordered the mass killing of sea otters. Many animals have been hunted to extinction in our country. You have a right to protest this practice by contacting environmental groups or by writing to federal or state legislators.

22. Using an almanac and other resources in the library media center, research an endangered animal or plant species and write proposed legislation to protect it. For example, you might write a law to restrict the hunting of sea otters off the coast of California. Consider the following issues: adequate reproduction versus overproduction of the species, uses of the sea otter, environmental protection, the importance of the sea otter in the food chain, predator–prey relationships, and preservation of the kelp beds. Are there additional ways to protect the sea otter? The National Geographic Society video *Seasons in the Sea* (Howard Hall Productions, 1990) provides detailed views of kelp beds and other marine environments. Look for this video and others in the library media center.

    Other endangered species that live in or near North America are the southern sea otter, the Florida panther, the red wolf, the American peregrine falcon, the bald eagle, the American alligator, and the American crocodile.

23. Fishing has changed little for millions of years. Describe a number of fishing practices. Compare the advantages and disadvantages of each practice, such as its effectiveness and how it affects or damages the marine environment. Some familiar methods of fishing are bait fishing with hook and line, commercial long lining, seining, spearing, harpooning, drift netting, trawling, fly casting, gigging, trapping, and shooting with bow and arrow. See chapter 12 for related activities.

24. Karana's primary source of food was the sea; she ate fish, scallops, kelp, and abalone. Consult a book about nutrition to learn the nutritional value of these foods. Compare seafood to beef, pork, and chicken. Compare calories and cholesterol as well as grams of fat, protein, and sodium. Martin Katahn's *One Meal at a Time* (New York: Warner Books, 1993) provides this information.

25. Kelp and other edible sea plants contain important nutrients, such as iodine. Dried seaweed can be purchased from some grocery stores or oriental shops. The following simple recipe can be prepared in the classroom.

    a. Soak 1 ounce of dried kelp in cold water overnight.

    b. Rinse the seaweed well and cut it into thin strips.

    c. Boil the seaweed in 4 cups of water 10 minutes, skimming the surface frequently.

    d. Drain well.

    e. Add 3 ounces of cooked, shredded pork or chicken.

    f. Season with 2 tablespoons of soy sauce, ½ teaspoon sugar, 1 teaspoon sesame oil, and a dash of salt.

26. The Channel Islands are surrounded by kelp beds. Kelp, a type of seaweed, is one of the sea's most valuable living resources. In the United States the kelp is used in manufacturing chemical products. Research the many ways seaweed is used in American industry.

27. Karana used natural objects to exploit her environment and use its resources. Find stones or shells that can be used as tools to open seashells, fillet fish, chop wood, scrape hides, and so forth. Find sticks to use as handles for the tools. Use heavy twine or leather shoelaces to tie the stones or shells to the handles. Display the tools with labels that describe their purpose. For an interesting contrast, display modern tools alongside the homemade ones.

28. Imagine that several items belonging to Karana have been found in a remote storage closet on San Nicholas. You have been commissioned to design a small museum dedicated to her life on the Island of the Blue Dolphins. Decide which items mentioned in the book may have been preserved, for example, her tools or feather skirt. Make a list of these items. Also list natural items that could be found on the island then and now, such as shells or rocks. From these lists, select items you will exhibit in your museum, and arrange the items into groups, or exhibits.

    Make a guidebook or pamphlet for the museum. Include a floor plan that indicates walls, doors, wall cases, display tables, dioramas, restrooms, ticket booths, snack areas, and natural displays, which may be outdoors. On the map indicate which items are in each display area. The exhibits and the pamphlet should reflect your understanding of the environment of the Channel Islands and the major events in *Island of the Blue Dolphins*. Be sure to name your museum and include tourist information in the pamphlet.

    Note: A pamphlet from a museum could give you many ideas for this project.

29. In *Island of the Blue Dolphins* the author makes many references to Karana's appearance and her clothing. Draw a picture of her for your museum pamphlet (activity 28), for a bulletin board display, or to illustrate a news article (activity 18).

30. Russian explorers crossed into North America and established many settlements on this continent. Research the history of the United States in the nineteenth century to see what areas of the United States were settled during the Russian exploration. How is their influence still in evidence, for example, in place names, such as the Russian River in northern California? Research the history of Alaska to complement what you find.

31.   *Zia* is the sequel to *Island of the Blue Dolphins.* Read the author's note in *Island of the Blue Dolphins* and predict how Karana's life continues before you read *Zia.*

32.   For more information about earthquakes, read "As the Earth Quakes . . . What Happens?" by Mohammed Hanif, in *Science and Children* (volume 27, number 4, January 1990). For information about earthquakes in California, read "Earthquake," by Thomas Canby, in *National Geographic* (volume 177, number 5, May 1990).

Related Titles

Canby, Thomas. "Earthquake." *National Geographic* 177, no. 5 (May 1990): 76-91.

Hanif, Mohammed. "As the Earth Quakes ... What Happens?" *Science and Children* 27, no. 4 (January 1990): 36-39.

Katahn, Martin. *One Meal at a Time*. New York: Warner Books, 1993.

A Thirteen/WNET Production. *Seasons in the Sea*. New York: Howard Hall Productions, National Geographic Society Videos, 1990.

Chapter 11
The Open Ocean

The Voyage of the Frog

Gary Paulsen
New York: Dell, 1989

Summary

Fourteen-year-old David sets sail from a marina at Ventura, California, with only one thought: to carry out his dying uncle's last request to scatter his ashes beyond the horizon. A sudden storm blows David off course, and David realizes that his supplies of food and fresh water are meager. David survives days of drifting, a sudden storm, a pod of killer whales, and a landing on the Baja California peninsula before he can set sail for home.

Earth Concepts

Oceans, weather, navigation, waves, map reading, salinity of oceans

Environmental Concepts

The individual in nature, scarcity and value of fresh water, predator and prey relationships, adaptation of marine animals

General Concepts

Sailing, boats, loyalty, determination, maritime folklore

Activities

1. To observe waves and regulate their speed in the classroom, use a 9-inch-by-12-inch glass or clear plastic tray. Clear salad containers from fast food restaurants serve well.

   a. Put a half inch of water in the tray.

   b. Using an eyedropper, drop one drop of water into the dish. Observe the effect.

   c. Slowly drop a sequence of drops into the dish. Observe the effect.

   d. Drop the water at a faster rate and observe the effect on the frequency of the waves.

   e. Experiment by altering the amount of water in the dish, the speed of the water drops, and the distance from the dropper to the dish. What variable causes more waves per second?

f.   Use two droppers, one at each end of the dish. Observe the effect.

Note: You can do this activity in small groups or as a class. To do the activity as a class, put the dish of water on an overhead projector.

2.   Waves are actually caused by wind. Repeat the previous activity, but instead of dropping water from an eyedropper, blow on the water through a soda straw. Blow very gently to produce the waves.

3.   To simulate the effect of wind on the sails of a boat, test how well various shapes of sails catch and hold the wind. You will need to do this activity on a pleasant but windy day.

   a.   Plant two poles 50 feet apart so that they are lined up with the wind. Or use two trees that are spaced and aligned correctly.

   b.   Stretch some monofilament nylon fish line between the poles.

   c.   String leaves or seed pods on the line at the windward end. Make a small tear in the leaves or seed pods to hook them on the line. Use a stopwatch to determine how long it takes for one object at a time to reach the other end of the line. Record the time for each object.

   d.   Determine the average time for each type of object. This will help determine which shapes best catch the wind.

   e.   Using paper or aluminum foil, make "faster-than-nature" objects that will travel the line faster than the natural objects. Test your objects on the line and compare their times with the times of natural objects.

4.   You have probably heard the expression "sailing the seven seas." Oceans and seas comprise more than 70 percent of the earth's surface.

   a.   Locate the oceans and seas on a globe. List them in order of their size, from smallest to largest. Check an almanac to see how you did.

   b.   Compare the total area of land on Earth to the total area of oceans by adding the square miles of each continent and each ocean and sea. You will find that all the continents can fit into one ocean. Trace the continents from a world map and cut them out. Try to fit them into one ocean. In which ocean do they fit?

5.   To investigate and map the ocean floor, see the activities in chapter 8.

6.   Sea water is very salty compared to fresh water. However, the concentration of salt in ocean water varies a great deal from one part of the ocean to another. In coastal bays in warmer regions, the water can be very salty because of evaporation. In the Arctic, where a considerable amount of ice melts, ocean water is less salty.
      Salt water is heavier, or more dense, than fresh water, because the salt molecules fit into the empty spaces between the water molecules. The principle of buoyancy states that objects float lower in lighter liquids and float higher in heavier liquids. Therefore, objects float higher in salt water than in fresh water. You can test the saltiness of water by how buoyant it is.

   a.   A hydrometer is an instrument used to measure the density of liquids. Make a simple hydrometer with a pencil, a thumbtack, and a tall, thin jar (see fig. 11.1). Stick the thumbtack into the eraser of a pencil. Fill the jar with water and place the pencil, eraser side down, in the water. Let the pencil float. If the pencil bottoms out, it is too heavy for the experiment. Remove some of the pencil with a pencil sharpener and continue.

b. Make five different salt solutions. Label them "A," "B," "C," and so on. Record the strength of each salt solution in a notebook. Remove the pencil, empty the jar, and refill it with solution A. Put the pencil in the water. Using a permanent marker, make a mark on the pencil at the water line and label the mark "A." Repeat this process for each salt solution. The pencil will have a series of marks on it, and you will know what the salt solution is for each mark. Now you have a hydrometer ready to test unknown concentrations.

c. Have someone in the class leave the room to make a salt solution. Put the solution in the jar, put the pencil in the water, and see if you can tell how strong the salt solution is.

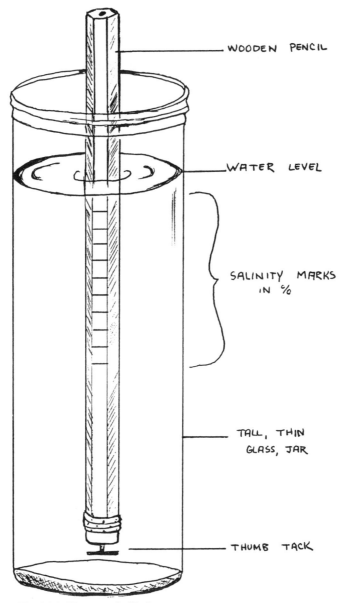

WOODEN PENCIL

WATER LEVEL

SALINITY MARKS IN %

TALL, THIN GLASS, JAR

THUMB TACK

Fig. 11.1. Homemade Hydrometer.

7. David constantly struggled to keep dry. You can demonstrate the basics of evaporation and compare the rate of evaporation for several different liquids.

   a. Use the black board as the test surface. Divide the blackboard into three areas. Label the areas Water, Rubbing Alcohol, and Nail Polish Remover.

   b. Place two milliliters each of water, rubbing alcohol, and nail polish remover into separate paper cups.

   c. Three volunteers take one of the paper cups and stand at the appropriate section of the blackboard. Three more volunteers with stopwatches stand beside them.

   d. At a signal from the teacher, each student applies the liquid to the blackboard using a cotton ball or cotton swab. The volunteers with stopwatches time how long it takes for each liquid to streak and disappear.

   e. The volunteers who applied the liquids to the blackboard describe how their hands felt as they applied the liquids. The cooling they felt indicates that heat is required for the process to occur.

   f. Discuss evaporation that you experience each day, such as using a hair dryer or drying clothes.

   This activity is adapted from "The Disappearing Act," by Lisa Gentile, in *Science and Children* (volume 28, number 8, May 1991).

8. David had very few supplies and no way to preserve food after it was opened. Discuss the ways food is preserved and packed. Make a list of nonperishable foods that you would take on a sailing trip. Include enough supplies to last four or five days. Also calculate the amount of fresh water you will need to take for drinking and cooking. Remember, there will be no refrigeration or fast food. Include on your list foods to provide well-balanced meals, and don't include a lot of junk food.

9. For sailors, clouds are an important indicator of the weather. Study the major cloud formations, then log the formations that are observed each day. Also log the weather conditions that accompany each kind of cloud. Use this information to predict the weather from cloud patterns. Working in three small groups, experiment with three ways to predict weather from cloud formations.

   Group one predicts the weather from clouds it observes.

   Group two predicts the weather from cloud formations shown on radar on a weather channel.

   Group three predicts the weather from cloud formations reported in a newspaper weather report or weather map.

   Compare the three methods to see which is most accurate.

10. There are many sayings and proverbs about weather and weather predictions, for example, "Red skies at night, sailor's delight; red skies in the morning, sailors take warning." Ask parents and other teachers whether they know any weather-related sayings. Check the *Farmer's Almanac* for weather-related sayings. Make a bulletin board display of the sayings with pictures of weather conditions and descriptive writing.

11. Use television and newspapers to study general weather conditions. Some resources are:

    - The Weather Channel (TWC) on cable television.
    - AccuWeather, a computer-based weather information service to which schools can subscribe. Contact AccuWeather, 619 West College Avenue, State College, PA 16801.
    - *Aviation Weather,* a weather forecast for pilots. It is aired on Public Broadcasting Service (PBS) stations in some areas at 7 a.m. each day.
    - Local television weather reports.
    - Local radio weather reports.
    - Local newspapers' weather reports.
    - The *USA Today* weather page.

    Watch or read local weather forecasts from two or more sources. Compare the forecasts' predictions of high and low pressure systems, types and positions of fronts, precipitation, sunny or cloudy areas, temperatures, and so forth. How accurate were the forecasts?

12. David encountered an oil tanker on his voyage. To demonstrate the best design of a tanker, see chapter 8.

13. Learn to read and draw angles from 0 degrees to 360 degrees by playing Navigation Game.

    a. The game board is flip-chart paper printed with a 1-inch or 2-inch grid. Label one side of the paper "NORTH" or "0 Degrees."

    b. Make a spinner and an angle plotter for each group by photocopying the compasses, spinner arrow, and protractor arm from figure 11.2A, page 136. To assemble, follow the directions on the figure.

    c. Working in groups of four to six, compete in a race from the center of the sheet to any outside edge. Each group will plot its course using a different color pencil or marker.

    d. One team's player spins the spinner to determine the angle to sail. Another player on the same team plots an angle from the spot in the center of the paper to a spot one square away from the starting point as shown in figure 11.2B, page 137. Then the player draws a line between the two points. The process of plotting the angle and drawing the line is shown in figure 11.3, page 138.

    e. Teams take turns, with each team member getting a chance to spin and plot a course.

    f. In subsequent turns, players plot newly spun angles to sail from the position they had previously attained. The first team to reach an edge of the paper wins.

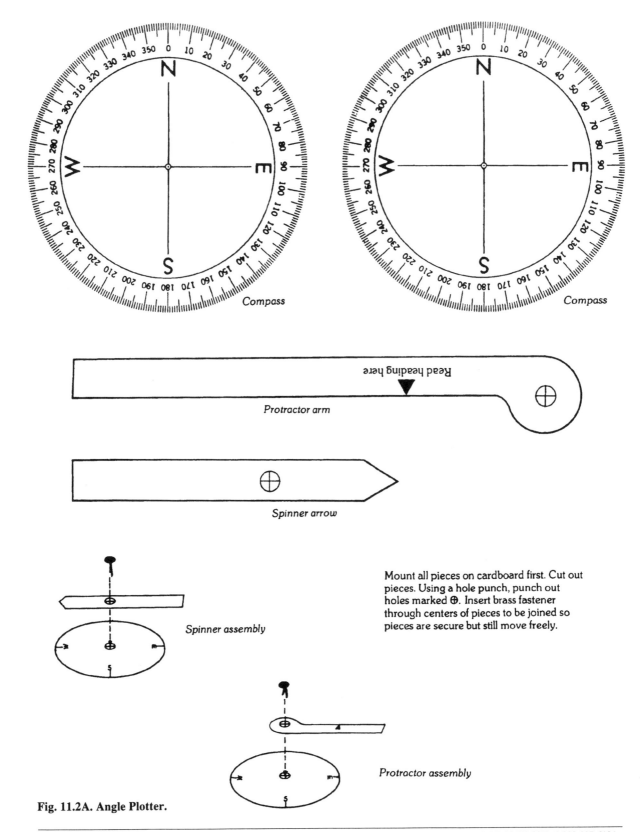

Compass

Compass

Read heading here

Protractor arm

Spinner arrow

Mount all pieces on cardboard first. Cut out pieces. Using a hole punch, punch out holes marked ⊕. Insert brass fastener through centers of pieces to be joined so pieces are secure but still move freely.

Spinner assembly

Protractor assembly

Fig. 11.2A. Angle Plotter.

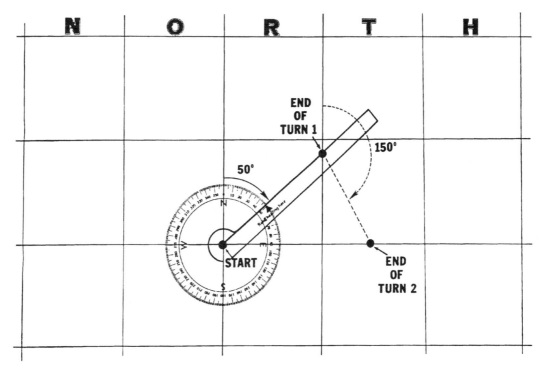

Fig. 11.2B. Using the Angle Plotter.

14. Play a variation of Navigation Game.

    a. Use the same game board, but place a cardboard arrow at the middle of one edge of the paper. The arrow should point to the center of the board. This indicates the wind direction. Wind direction remains constant throughout the game.

    b. Instead of beginning play at the center of the board, begin at the middle of the edge of the board opposite the wind arrow. Home port is the wind arrow.

    c. Working in teams, one player throws a die to determine the number of squares to be moved. Play may be in any direction but must be 45 degrees to the wind.

    d. To get to home port you must sail in a zigzag pattern called tacking.

15. Another variation on Navigation Game uses a marine chart as a game board. Cover the chart with a sheet of clear plastic for drawing. Longitude and latitude lines form the grid, and of course north is marked on the chart. This game has the added challenge of navigating around land masses and islands.

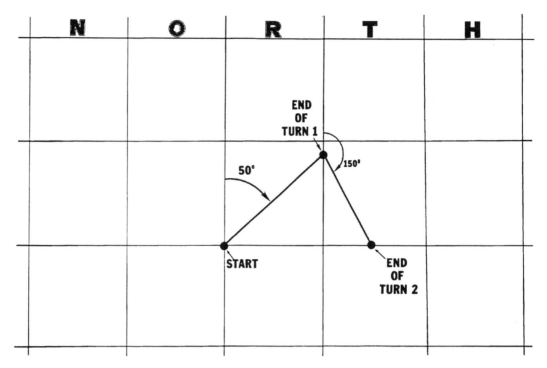

Fig. 11.3. Playing the Navigation Game.

16. *The Voyage of the Frog* contains a line drawing of the parts of a sailing vessel. Figure 11.4 shows several parts of a single vessel. Become familiar with these parts of vessels so that you will recognize the purpose of each part as you read *The Voyage of the Frog*. Which part of the boat is used to help propel or control the course of the boat in the wind? Which parts are designed to accelerate the boat or to slow its progress? What must the sailor do with the sail as the direction of the wind changes? Which parts of the sail can be moved by the sailor and which parts are stationary?

17. Popular magazines, such as *Yachting* and *Cruising* publish interesting and informative articles about boats and the art of navigation as well as descriptions of voyages to all parts of the world. Read some articles for pleasure or use them as sources of ideas and information for projects. Ask the library media specialist to obtain some copies of these magazines and books on ships and sailing.

18. Compare the line drawing of the boat in *The Voyage of the Frog* to pictures of sailboats in magazines. Why do the shapes of the boats' hulls vary? Why does the rigging of the sails differ? How do the forms of power used by modern sailboats differ from the forms of power used on boats in the past, for example, the ancient Greek and Phoenician boats, the Elizabethan buccaneer boats, or the ships of Columbus and the Pilgrims? Use resources in the library media center to find information about sailing ships throughout history. Display a time line of ship silhouettes on a bulletin board.

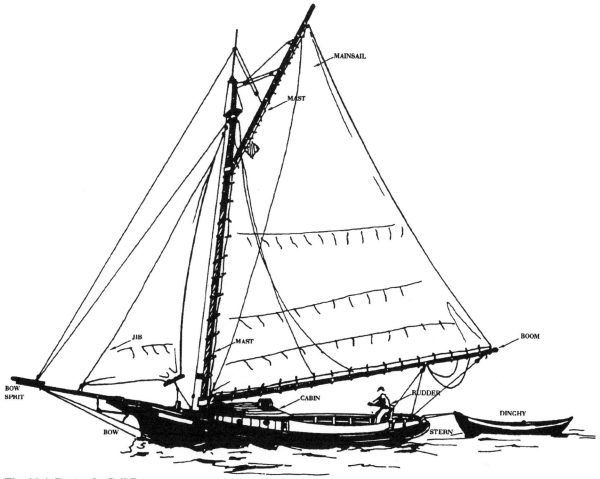

Fig. 11.4. Parts of a Sail Boat.

19. Pretend you own a large sailing vessel that sleeps fifteen passengers and a crew of three. Groups charter your boat for fishing expeditions or sailing between islands in the Caribbean. Write an advertisement for a sailing magazine to promote your boat and your services. Be sure to include the name of your business, the home port, how customers can contact you, and any information that would attract customers. Look at advertisements in sailing magazines to see how they are written. Include a drawing of your ship.

20. The main theme of *The Voyage of the Frog* is David's determination to keep his promise to Uncle Owen. All of us are asked to keep promises. Write about a promise you kept and tell whether it was easy or difficult. You do not have to reveal the promise if it is personal. Write about how you feel when you are faced with a difficult task or choice.

21. You can make small boats from sheets of styrofoam packing, popsicle sticks, chopsticks, or fast food containers. The object of this activity is to make a boat to sail across a wading pool. A fan turned on very low speed provides the wind to propel the boats. You can stage races with several boats competing at once or with individual timed trials. If boats are sailed singularly, a wallpaper wetting trough can be used as the container.

To stage a School Cup race, compete in elimination races until only two contestants are left. Divide the class into two teams, one for each boat. Each group experiments with adding design features to make the boat sail faster. Students who do not wish to be on a boat's team may design the trophy or provide commentary during the final race.

For additional ideas, read "Wading Pool Regatta," by Robert McDonald, in *Science and Children,* (volume 27, number 6, March 1990).

22. It is said that to the save the earth we must save the oceans. Discuss this concept. Then design posters, make commercials, write rap lyrics, or find another way to express how you feel about saving the earth and oceans. Post your projects on a hallway bulletin board for other students to see.

23. David landed on Mexico's Baja California peninsula. Using a map of this area from the atlas and information from the book, where do you think he was? Calculate the latitude and longitude of his position. By referring to vegetation, precipitation, landform and population maps, what would you expect the area to look like? What are the chances that someone would be there to assist David? What food sources might he find?

24. Using the small map in *The Voyage of the Frog,* calculate the distance from Ventura, California, to Baja California, Mexico, and back to Ventura. Using maps of wind patterns and ocean currents from a science book or encyclopedia, predict how the winds and currents will affect his trip. If David sails an average of 7 knots per hour, how long will the trip take, assuming no detours or problems arise? Note: A knot equals 1 nautical mile per hour or 6075 feet (1.852 km) per hour.

25. Killer whales often are maligned because of false information about them. Research orcas in your library media center. An excellent picture book is Vicki Leon's *A Pod of Killer Whales,* (San Luis Obispo, CA: Blake Publishing, 1989; 800-727-8558).

Related Titles

Gentile, Lisa. "The Disappearing Act." *Science and Children* 28 no. 8 (May 1991): 26-27.

Leon, Vicki. *A Pod of Killer Whales*. San Luis Obispo, CA: Blake Publishing, 1989.

McDonald, Robert. "Wading Pool Regatta." *Science and Children* 27, no. 6 (March 1990): 16-17.

Chapter 12
Whales and Marine Fishing

The Hostage
Theodore Taylor
New York: Dell, 1987

Summary

Jamie and his family live in a remote fishing community on the Pacific coast of British Columbia. Salmon fishing, Jamie's father's occupation, provides money for few modern conveniences and no tuition for Jamie to attend boarding school. When a killer whale is trapped in a small inlet, the family must decide whether to sell the animal to Sea Shows, Inc. for $100,000 or set it free.

Earth Concepts

Rain forests and trees, land–sea relationships, landforms, oceans, weather and fog

Environmental Concepts

Predator–prey relationships, conservation of wildlife, fisheries, regulations, gill netting, environmental organizations, animals as entertainment

General Concepts

Sea animals, economics of fishing, fishing techniques, animal rights, coastal lifestyle, whale life cycle, salmon life cycle

Activities

1. Many of the places in *The Hostage* actually exist. On a road map of British Columbia find the city of Vancouver and Vancouver Island with its cities, Victoria and Port Hardy. Calvert Island is close to Jamie's home on the Fitz Hugh Sound. Note the relative locations of the Queen Charlotte Islands and the city of Prince Rupert to the U.S. cities of Seattle, Washington, and Juneau, Alaska. Read books about British Columbia to learn more about this land.

141

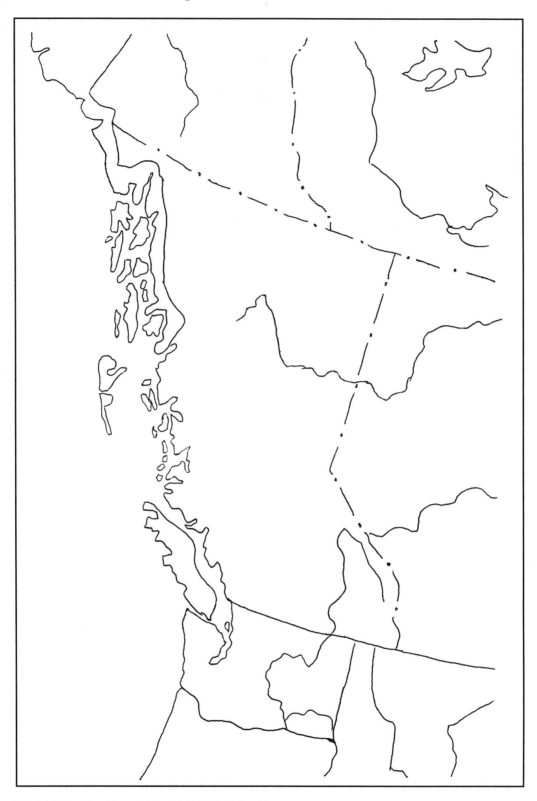

Fig. 12.1. Outline Map of Coastal British Columbia.

2. Wilwilli Cove and Lumber Landing are fictional places. However, by comparing the map in *The Hostage* with a map of British Columbia you can determine exactly where the story takes place. Note the name of the village in this area.

3. Jamie's father makes his living as a salmon fisherman. Laws and regulations restrict him to specific fishing dates and seasons because there are few salmon in this area. Many factors contribute to the short supply of salmon. Consider the life cycle of salmon and its hazards.

   - Eggs and immature fish must struggle to live in polluted fresh water.

   - As growing fish migrate downriver to the sea, they must maneuver around dams and obstacles.

   - Adult fish may be caught by huge factory ships spread around the ocean.

   - Mature fish migrating upstream to spawn and lay their eggs must maneuver around dams and obstacles.

In small groups discuss these and other problems in the salmon life cycle. Develop laws or procedures to help the salmon survive.

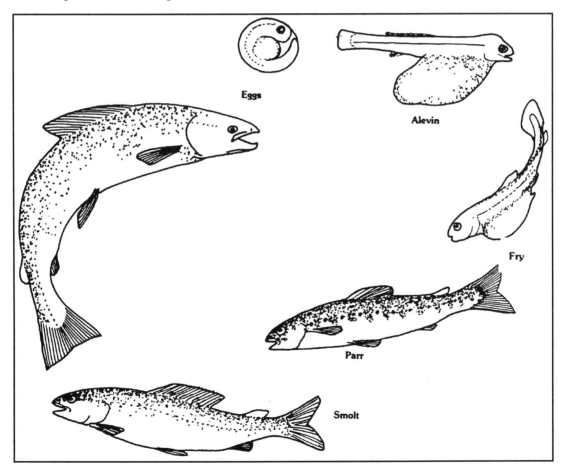

Fig. 12.2. Life Cycle of Salmon.

4. Jamie's father used a method of fishing called gill netting. The fisherman anchors one end of the net to the ocean floor and stretches it to the surface of the ocean. After some hours, the fisherman hauls in the net and the trapped fish. Other methods of commercial fishing (illustrated in fig. 12.3) are:

- purse seining, in which a large net floats near the surface of the water. When a school of fish is enclosed in the net, the net is drawn up.

- otter trawling, in which a cone-shaped net with wooden doors is towed through the water.

- longlining, in which many baited hooks are attached to a line that is up to several miles long. The line is set between two buoys, and after several hours it is reeled in.

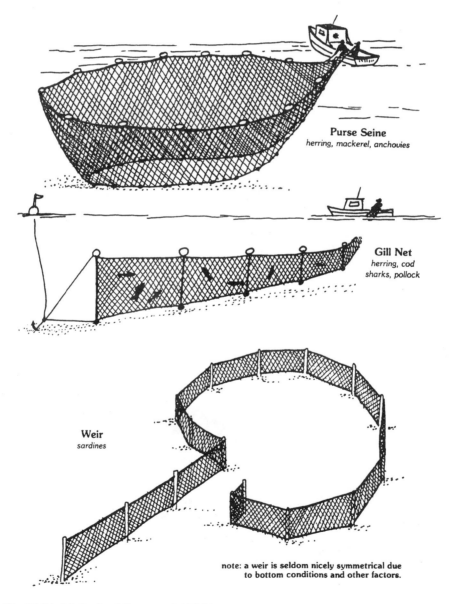

Purse Seine
herring, mackerel, anchovies

Gill Net
herring, cod
sharks, pollock

Weir
sardines

note: a weir is seldom nicely symmetrical due to bottom conditions and other factors.

Fig. 12.3A. Methods of Commercial Fishing.

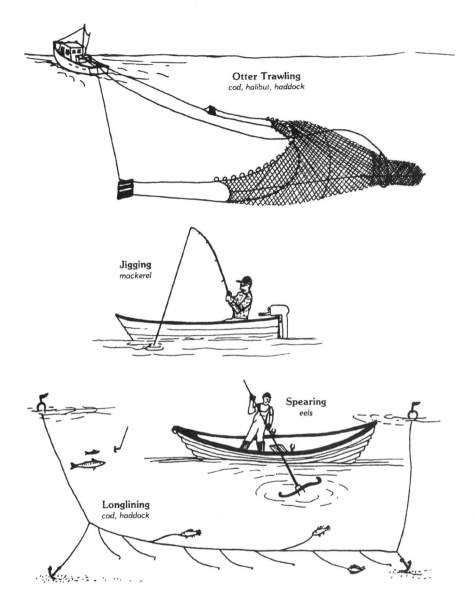

Fig. 12.3B. Methods of Commercial Fishing.

Form small discussion groups to study methods of fishing, including the advantages and disadvantages of each and whether they are environmentally sound. Consider:

a. If this device gets lost, will it catch fish without the control of the fisherman?

b. Will the device entrap marine mammals, such as whales and seals?

c. Does using the device require a great deal of energy?

d. Does the device require a great deal of hand work to prepare and use it?

5. Many species of salmon are eaten. Check the canned goods and the fresh fish sections of a supermarket to learn the names of the species. Compute the cost per ounce of the canned varieties. Find out the cost per pound for fresh salmon. Convert the cost per ounce to cost per pound so you can compare the prices. Ask a sales clerk about the species, source, and availability of salmon sold in the store.

6. The humpback whale is a favorite prey of the killer whale, even though the humpback is the bigger of the two. Because they are so often attacked, the tails of humpback whales bear markings unique to each animal. Scientists take photographs of individual humpback whale's tails as the animals sound, or dive. The photos are used to study the individual whales as they migrate. You can simulate this process using pictures of humpback whales' tails. The object of the simulation is to match the pictures and locations on the cards to determine whether individual whales have been sighted more than once. Note: The whole tail pictures are artistic renderings of actual living animals. This authentic data is from the east coast of North America. Similar migrations are noted for humpbacked whales on the west coast as well.

   a. Work in groups to make whale tail cards. Figure 12.4, pages 147-49, shows several whales' tails. Make several photocopies of the figure, cut out the tails, and paste each one on an index card. Each card represents one sighting of the whale.

   b. Working with your team, lay the cards face up on a table. Decide which cards show the same whale's tail. Place all the cards for each whale in separate piles. Then plot the sightings of each whale on a map of the North Atlantic Ocean (see fig. 12.4D, p. 150). Use a different color to represent each whale.

   c. After plotting the whale sightings, describe the movements of each whale. Do they seem to have home territories? Do they migrate?

   d. Humpback whale tails often bear herringbone marks made by the teeth of killer whales. Which pictures show evidence of an attack by killer whales?

7. The theme of *The Hostage* is whether it is right to capture animals and sell them to parks and zoos for the amusement of people. Animal rights activists are leaders in the movement to stop this exploitation of animals. However, many animals are already in captivity in zoos, theme parks, and aquariums. Should it be illegal to capture wild animals for amusement? What about animals that are already captured? Rather than discuss this issue, stage a role play called Free Shamu! Characters in the role play might be zookeepers, theme park owners, animal rights activists, wildlife experts, educators, parents and children, environmentalists, and oceanographers. Role play one of these characters and state your views.

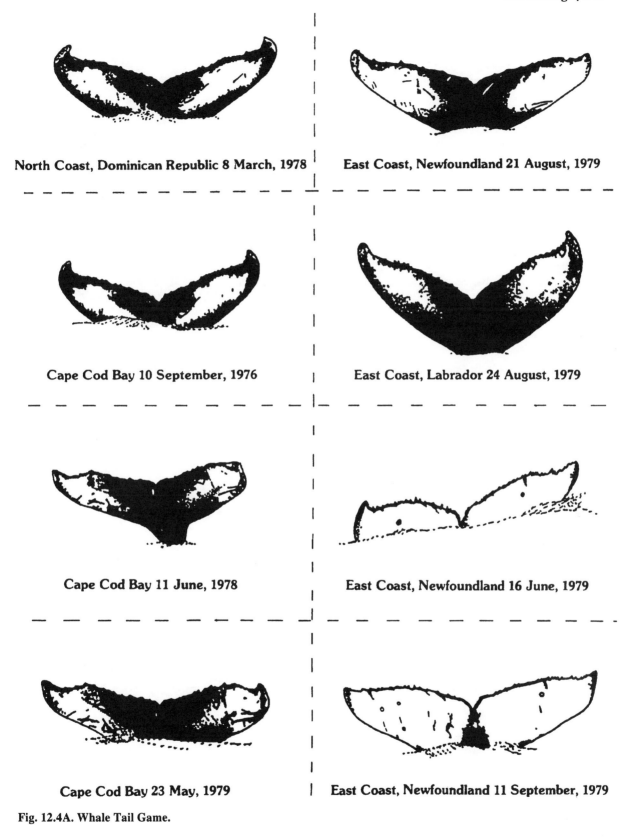

North Coast, Dominican Republic 8 March, 1978

East Coast, Newfoundland 21 August, 1979

Cape Cod Bay 10 September, 1976

East Coast, Labrador 24 August, 1979

Cape Cod Bay 11 June, 1978

East Coast, Newfoundland 16 June, 1979

Cape Cod Bay 23 May, 1979

East Coast, Newfoundland 11 September, 1979

Fig. 12.4A. Whale Tail Game.

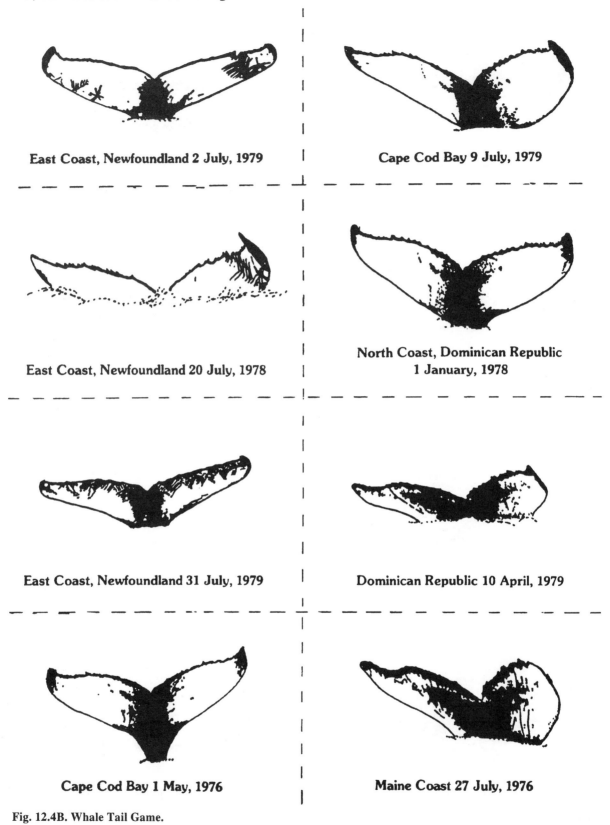

East Coast, Newfoundland 2 July, 1979

Cape Cod Bay 9 July, 1979

East Coast, Newfoundland 20 July, 1978

North Coast, Dominican Republic
1 January, 1978

East Coast, Newfoundland 31 July, 1979

Dominican Republic 10 April, 1979

Cape Cod Bay 1 May, 1976

Maine Coast 27 July, 1976

Fig. 12.4B. Whale Tail Game.

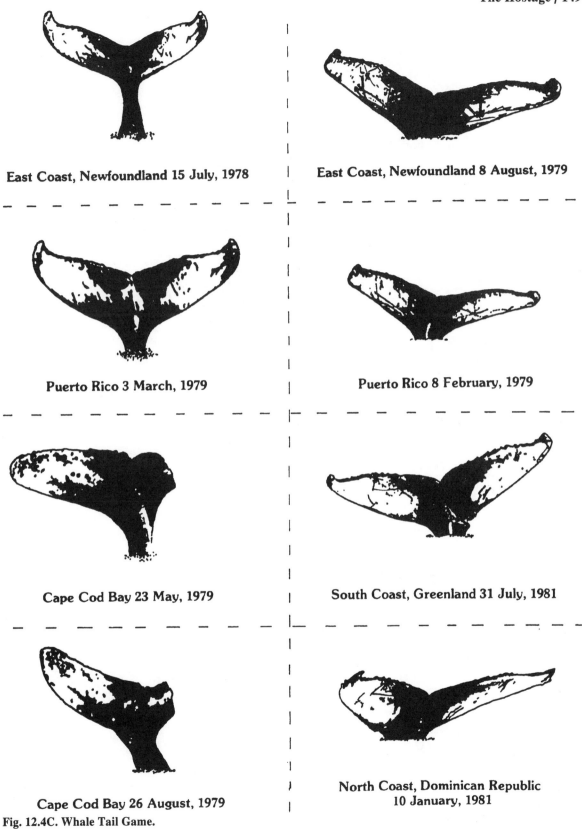

East Coast, Newfoundland 15 July, 1978

East Coast, Newfoundland 8 August, 1979

Puerto Rico 3 March, 1979

Puerto Rico 8 February, 1979

Cape Cod Bay 23 May, 1979

South Coast, Greenland 31 July, 1981

Cape Cod Bay 26 August, 1979

North Coast, Dominican Republic 10 January, 1981

Fig. 12.4C. Whale Tail Game.

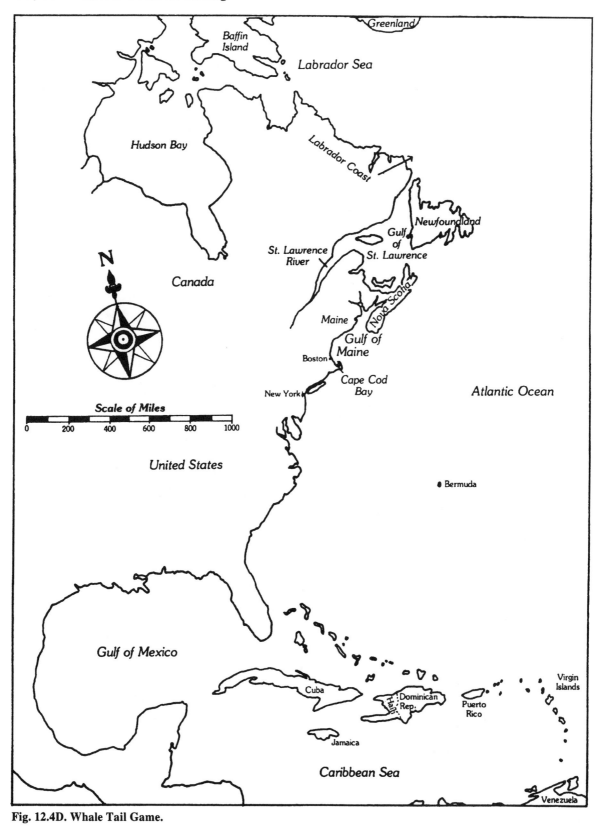

Fig. 12.4D. Whale Tail Game.

8. Most people have many misconceptions about the nature of killer whales. Ask the library media specialist to help you find books about killer whales. Using what you learn compose ten true or false statements about killer whales. Reproduce several copies of the list and distribute it to both students and adults. Ask them to indicate whether each statement is true or false. Compare students' answers to adults' answers. Some simple statements about killer whales are:

> Killer whales are very large dolphins often called orcas.

> Whales can grow so large that Native Americans used their bones to build the framework of homes and boats.

> All killer whales are vicious meat eaters.

> Killer whales seek out humans as their prey.

(The first two statements are true and the last two are false.) Or, create a survey about killer whales similar to the survey about wolves in chapter 4.

9. Trawler Man is a board game that simulates a day in the life of a fisherman. The object of the game is to see how much money you can make from fishing. Figure 12.5, pages 152-57, includes the board used to play the game along with the game cards. The game begins and ends at the mooring. The rules are:

- The person with the highest number on the throw of the dice begins.

- Each player takes turns throwing the dice and moving the number of spaces indicated. Each player follows the instructions on the square on which he or she lands.

- If the player lands on a space in the fishing grounds, a fish-catch card is drawn.

- If the player lands on a space that is already occupied, the player must immediately roll again and move *backward* the number of spaces indicated by the second roll.

- When the first boat reaches the mooring, the game is over. All boats must immediately go to the mooring.

- Each player totals his or her catch and calculates its dollar value. The player with the greatest dollar value wins.

Trawlerman

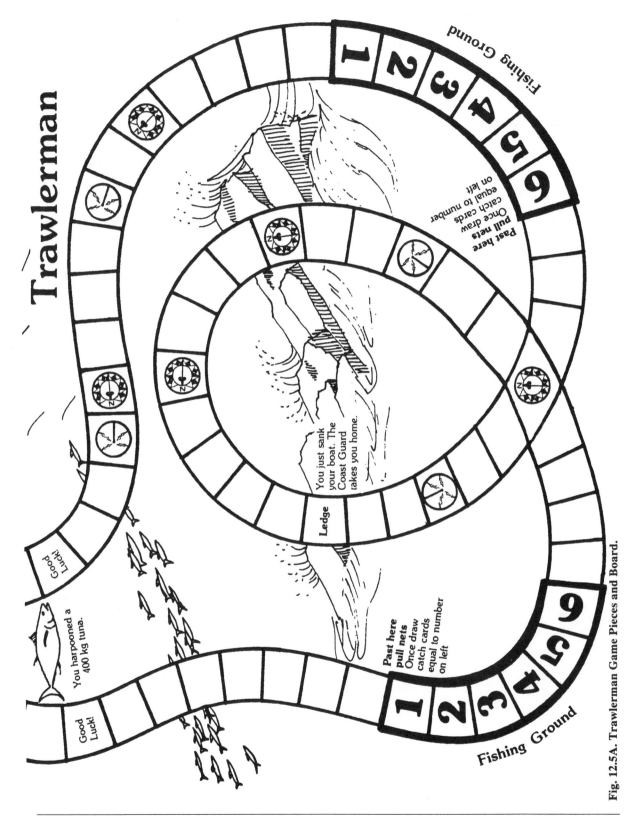

On the board:

Fishing Ground
1 2 3 4 5 6

Past here pull nets Once draw catch cards equal to number on left

You just sank your boat. The Coast Guard takes you home.

Ledge

Past here pull nets Once draw catch cards equal to number on left

Fishing Ground
1 2 3 4 5 6

Good Luck!

You harpooned a 400 kg tuna.

Good Luck!

Fig. 12.5A. Trawlerman Game Pieces and Board.

Fishing Ground

1 2 3 4 5 6

Past here
pull nets
Once
draw
catch
cards
equal to
number
on left

Catch cards
here

Fisherman's Luck
cards here

Radio Check
cards here

Ledge

You were half asleep and
failed to keep to the proper
side of the buoy. You sank!

Mooring

Fishing Ground

1 2 3 4 5 6

Past
here
Pull nets
Once draw
catch cards
equal to number
on left

Fig. 12.5B. Trawlerman Game Pieces and Board.

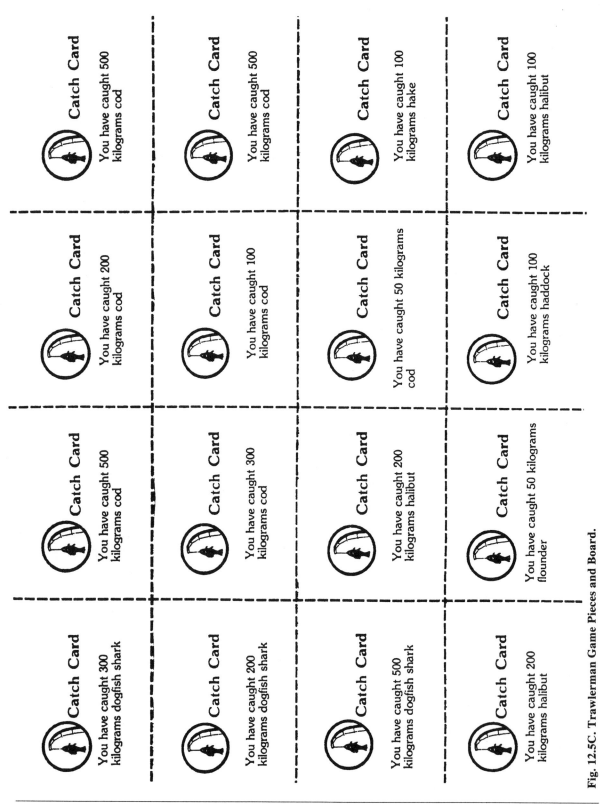

Fig. 12.5C. Trawlerman Game Pieces and Board.

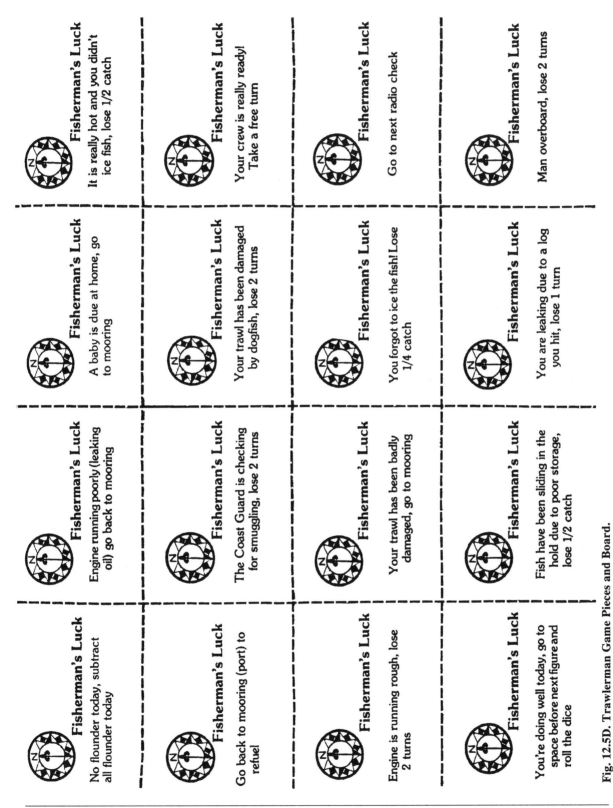

Fisherman's Luck
It is really hot and you didn't ice fish, lose 1/2 catch

Fisherman's Luck
Your crew is really ready! Take a free turn

Fisherman's Luck
Go to next radio check

Fisherman's Luck
Man overboard, lose 2 turns

Fisherman's Luck
A baby is due at home, go to mooring

Fisherman's Luck
Your trawl has been damaged by dogfish, lose 2 turns

Fisherman's Luck
You forgot to ice the fish! Lose 1/4 catch

Fisherman's Luck
You are leaking due to a log you hit, lose 1 turn

Fisherman's Luck
Engine running poorly (leaking oil) go back to mooring

Fisherman's Luck
The Coast Guard is checking for smuggling, lose 2 turns

Fisherman's Luck
Your trawl has been badly damaged, go to mooring

Fisherman's Luck
Fish have been sliding in the hold due to poor storage, lose 1/2 catch

Fisherman's Luck
No flounder today, subtract all flounder today

Fisherman's Luck
Go back to mooring (port) to refuel

Fisherman's Luck
Engine is running rough, lose 2 turns

Fisherman's Luck
You're doing well today, go to space before next figure and roll the dice

Fig. 12.5D. Trawlerman Game Pieces and Board.

From *Intermediate Science Through Children's Literature*, © 1994. Teacher Ideas Press, P.O. Box 6633, Englewood, CO 80155-6633. 1-800-237-6124.

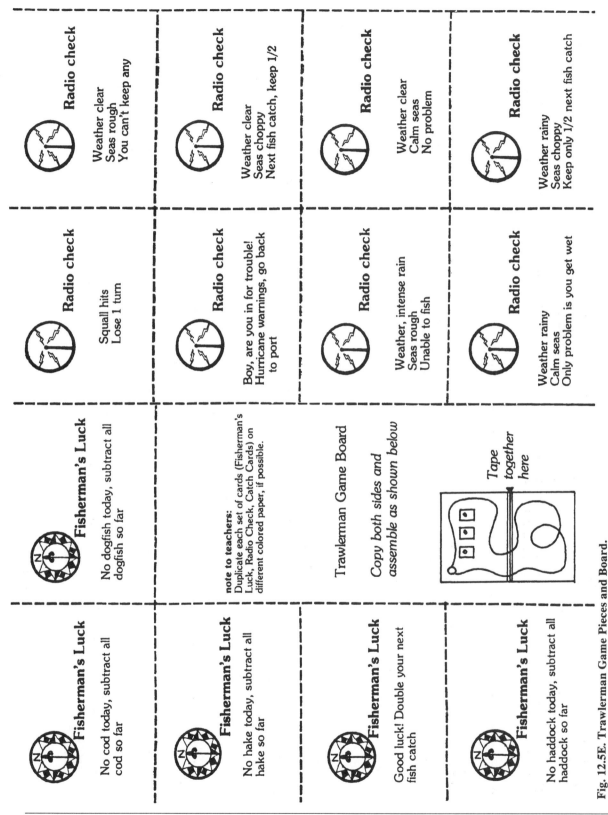

Radio check — Weather clear / Seas rough / You can't keep any

Radio check — Weather clear / Seas choppy / Next fish catch, keep 1/2

Radio check — Weather clear / Calm seas / No problem

Radio check — Weather rainy / Seas choppy / Keep only 1/2 next fish catch

Radio check — Squall hits / Lose 1 turn

Radio check — Boy, are you in for trouble! / Hurricane warnings, go back to port

Radio check — Weather, intense rain / Seas rough / Unable to fish

Radio check — Weather rainy / Calm seas / Only problem is you get wet

Fisherman's Luck — No dogfish today, subtract all dogfish so far

Fisherman's Luck — No cod today, subtract all cod so far

Fisherman's Luck — No hake today, subtract all hake so far

Fisherman's Luck — Good luck! Double your next fish catch

Fisherman's Luck — No haddock today, subtract all haddock so far

note to teachers: Duplicate each set of cards (Fisherman's Luck, Radio Check, Catch Cards) on different colored paper, if possible.

Trawlerman Game Board

Copy both sides and assemble as shown below

Tape together here

Fig. 12.5E. Trawlerman Game Pieces and Board.

Catch Tally Sheet

Species	Kilogram value in cents. This will vary and you may adjust the prices if you wish.	
Cod	$.40 kg.	
Haddock	$.80 kg.	
Hake	$.30 kg.	
Halibut	$3.00 kg.	
Flounder	$.60 kg.	
Dogfish shark throw the die if ≥4 no market today so no money.	$.20 kg.	
Tuna	$3.50 kg.	

Fig. 12.5E. Trawlerman Game Pieces and Board.

10. Most people think rain forests exist only in tropical areas, but the combination of the warm Japanese ocean current, and the geography of the Pacific Northwest—very narrow coastal regions rimmed by high volcanic mountains—make conditions right for rain forests in the state of Washington and the province of British Columbia. Westerly winds push warm ocean air up against the mountains. As the air is lifted, it rapidly cools, which causes it to drop a great deal of rain and snow on the coast. You can simulate the growing conditions of a rain forest in a large, clear, plastic container.

a. Make a 2-inch-square opening in the side of the container.

b. Place a 2-inch layer of potting soil on the bottom of the container. Plant peas, beans, squash, and radish seeds.

c. Seal the container.

d. Place the container where it will get sun each day.

e. Each day open the 2-inch-square opening and spray a fine mist of water into the container. Reseal the container.

Compare the growing conditions of a rain forest to normal growing conditions. Plant seeds in a plastic tray. Use the same kind of soil and the same kinds of seeds used in the simulated rain forest. Place the tray in the sun next to the simulated rain forest. Water the plants normally. Compare plants grown in the simulated rain forest with plants grown in normal conditions.

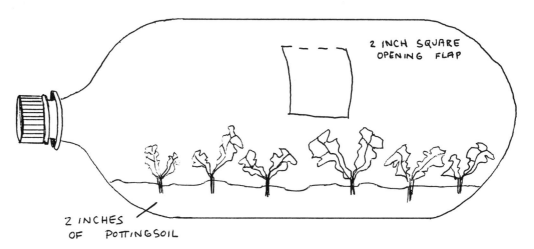

Fig. 12.6. Terrarium Rain Forest.

11. The northwest coast of North America is one of the wettest places in the hemisphere because of the combination of the warm Japanese ocean current and the geography of the Pacific Northwest—very narrow coastal regions rimmed by high volcanic mountains. Investigate these conditions by studying the relationship of water temperature to evaporation.

a. Use six plastic tumblers that are the same size. Put 1 cup of water in each tumbler.

b. Identify six locations with different temperatures. The locations may be inside or outside the classroom. Place one tumbler in each location. Record the temperature in that location.

c. After several hours collect the tumblers. Pour the water from a tumbler into a measuring cup or graduated cylinder. Subtract the amount of water remaining from the amount of water you had at the start (1 cup) to determine how much water evaporated from that tumbler. Do this for each tumbler.

d. For each tumbler calculate the percentage of water that evaporated. Graph the percentage of evaporation versus the temperature. Is there a clear relationship between water temperature and evaporation? How does that relate to conditions prevailing along the northwest coast of North America?

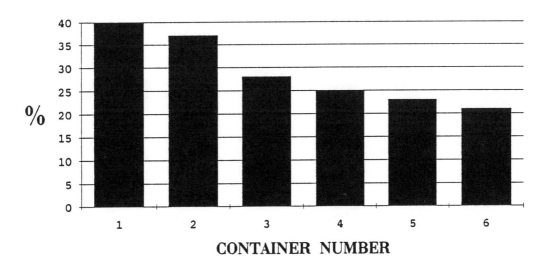

Fig. 12.7. Graph of Temperature versus Evaporation Rate.

12. Investigate temperature and precipitation using a shiny metal can.

a. Fill the can half full of water. Insert a thermometer in the water as shown in figure 12.8, page 160.

b. Observe the temperature as you slowly add ice cubes to the water.

c. When a film of water begins to appear on the outside of the can, record the water temperature.

d. Discuss the source of the water that appears on the outside of the can.

e. The temperature measured when water appeared on the outside of the can is the dew point for this experiment. The dew point is the temperature at which rain or other precipitation begins to form. The dew point may be a different temperature under various conditions.

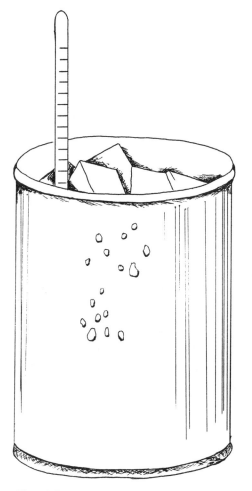

Fig. 12.8. Dew Point Activity Apparatus.

13. Harvesting spruce, fir and hemlock was a traditional occupation in British Columbia. For activities regarding the timber industry, see chapter 5.

14. British Columbia has more land area than Texas but only 20 percent of the population. Most people in British Columbia live close to the U.S. border. Use information from encyclopedias and other books to formulate a reasonable explanation for this.

15. Jamie led a very isolated life. Make a list to compare your life to his, including school, chores, shopping for food or clothing, use of electricity, television viewing, contact with peers, and so forth. If you were to change places with Jamie, what would be the most difficult adjustment? What would you enjoy the most?

16. How would the viewing habits of your family be affected if your family had a generator or a battery-powered television? Write down each family member's favorite programs and how long they are. Assume that the family has only one television and that viewing must be limited to two hours per day. Allot a certain number of hours to each person per week. Establish a schedule that best suits each family member. What do you think will happen? Will people watch programs together? Will some people offer to trade their

television viewing time for activities (such as doing the chores) or objects? Will someone insist on watching a program that no one else likes, or will everyone cooperate? How will you spend the spare time that can no longer be spent watching television?

17. Many people who earn their living on the sea wear insulated, waterproof clothing to guard against hypothermia. Hypothermia occurs when the body loses much of its heat; the heart rate, pulse, and responsiveness to light fade, and the person eventually dies. Hypothermia can result from exposure to ocean water that is cooler than the body's temperature. Explore how hypothermia works.

    a. Dissolve unflavored gelatin in water. Divide the gelatin among several small, self-sealing plastic bags. Allow the gelatin to set. For the purposes of this experiment, the gelatin behaves almost exactly like a human body.

    b. After the gelatin sets, open the bags and place a thermometer inside the gelatin in each one. Reseal the bags.

    c. Fill several large containers with water at various temperatures at or below room temperature.

    e. Submerge one bag in each container.

    f. Observe the temperature change inside each bag. How quickly does the temperature drop? How does the temperature inside the bag compare with the temperature of the water surrounding it? Assuming that a 10-degree drop would kill the "gelatin bag creatures," how many creatures were able to survive?

    g. Design a survival suit that would protect the gelatin bag creature from the cold water. The suit must be a good insulator and waterproof. Repeat the experiment with the survival suits. Did more gelatin bag creatures survive?

18. Many species of fish are called salmon. Salmon species include chinook, sockeye, chum, coho, and humpback (pink). Most of the world's salmon species live along the east and west coasts of the north Pacific. Using resources in the library media center, find pictures of each salmon species. Create a full-size picture of each salmon species. Which of the species are raised commercially? Which are sought by sport fishermen in areas where the species are *not* indigenous? Create a bulletin board display using the drawings of the species and additional information gathered in the library media center.

19. Several national and international organizations work for wildlife preservation. The groups differ greatly in organizational structure as well as practices and areas of special concern. Contact one or more of these groups to learn more about their goals and methods. Some organizations are Greenpeace, the Sierra Club, the Audubon Society, and the National Wildlife Federation. If a wildlife group has a chapter or affiliate in your area, invite a representative to speak to your class.

20. Visit a zoo or animal park. Carefully observe the conditions in which the animals live and are displayed. Are these conditions similar to the animal's natural habitat? What provisions are made for the animals' comfort? How are their dietary and medical needs addressed? Do animals reproduce in captivity? Are there any endangered species represented? Are they given special care? Formulate other questions before you visit the zoo or park.

21. Native American stories and legends are an important part of the culture of western British Columbia. Ask your library media specialist to help you find some stories from Native Americans in this part of the continent. *Keepers of the Animals,* by Michael J. Caduto and Joseph Bruchac (Golden, CO: Fulcrum Press, 1991) contains three stories from Pacific Northwest Native Americans: "Salmon Boy," "The Woman Who Married a Frog," and "Octopus and Raven."

Fig. 12.9. Box Totem Poles.

22. Native Americans of the Pacific Northwest include the Nootka, the Squamish, the Quileute, the Haida, and the Kwakiutl. Research these groups and compare their cultures and living conditions with one another or with Native American groups in your area.

23. One of the most unique features of the Pacific Northwest is the totem pole, which tells the story of a tribe. Consult your art teacher for information on these sculptures, or gather information in the library media center. Draw or carve a statue. Or, build a totem pole using cardboard boxes decorated to resemble animals. Use construction paper or tempera paint to decorate the boxes, then stack the boxes and glue them together.

24. The theme of the movie *Free Willie* (Warner Brothers, 1993) is similar to the theme of *The Hostage.* Watch *Free Willie* and compare the two stories. If you like, debate the issue that the stories present.

References

Schools can obtain educational material about killer whales and marine animals from Sea World, which has locations in Orlando, Florida; San Diego, California; and Aurora, Ohio. Request the materials several weeks before beginning this unit.

Related Titles

Caduto, Michael J., and Joseph Bruchac. *Keepers of the Animals: Native American Stories & Wildlife Activities for Children.* Golden, CO: Fulcrum, 1991.

Free Willie. Produced by Jennie Lew Tugend. Burbank, CA: Warner Brothers, 1993, videocassette.

Chapter 13
Freshwater Lakes

The Island
Gary Paulsen
New York: Dell, 1988

Summary

Wil Neuton's island in a small lake in northern Wisconsin became a refuge from the realities of adolescent turmoil. Aided by a friend who replenished food supplies, Wil found that the beauties of nature were far preferable to the town that was his new home. Still, he could not prevent civilization from encroaching on him, nor could the impasse with his father last forever.

Earth Concepts

Lake evolution, glacier to lake to bog progression, physical characteristics of a lake, temperature zones of water, lake beaches

Environmental Concepts

Plants and animals, relation of plants and animals to temperature zones of lakes, movement of animals, food chain, human manipulation of the environment, love of nature, preservation of the environment

General Concepts

Techniques of observation, writing, interpersonal relationships, need for solitude

Activities

1. Wil, the story's main character, lives near Sucker Lake in Wisconsin. This fictitious lake is similar to Escanaba Lake, which is in Vilas County, Wisconsin. Before you begin to study *The Island,* purchase copies of topographical maps and a key that explains their symbols. Sources and other materials are listed in the resources section at the end of this chapter.

2. Read the prologue of *The Island* two or three times, then draw a map of the island based on the description of it. Indicate the island's size, shape, orientation, vegetation, rocks, bays, and other natural features. As you read the book, add details or alterations to your map. After you finish the book, make a final copy of your map using colors or symbols to

indicate the various features. Compare the island to a similarly shaped one in Escanaba Lake.

3. From your map of the island and *The Island,* you will have a general knowledge about the lake bottom and the turbidity of the water. Deduce how the lake was formed, its age, and the source of its water.

4. You can make a three-dimensional model of the bottom of Escanaba Lake using the topographical map in figure 13.1. Make as many copies of the map as there are contour lines. Using the copies, cut out patterns, one along each contour line. You should end up with a stack of patterns that corresponds to the shape and depth of the lake bottom. Using the patterns cut the shapes from cardboard, oak tag, balsa wood, thin styrofoam, or another sturdy material. Stack these sturdy pieces in the same order they appear on the map to make a model of Lake Escanaba. The deepest contour is on the bottom; the shallowest on top.

Figure 13.1A. Lake Bottom Profile: Depth Is Given in Feet.

Fig. 13.1B. Three-dimensional Model of Lake Bottom.

5. Compare the islands on the topographical map of Escanaba Lake with the one you drew based on the description in *The Island.* Compare the size and shape, islands, water depth, lake bottom, and surrounding territory of the two lakes.

6. Escanaba Lake and Sucker Lake are glacier lakes. To see how a glacier can change the earth's surface, see activity ten in chapter 6. Note: Glacier lakes eventually disappear if there is no inflow or continuous source of water.

7. Select a lake near your home. Obtain a USGS topographical map or a lake-depth map from the state department of conservation or natural resources. Compare the lake near your home with Sucker Lake. How are they similar? How are they different?

8. Many people think that lakes and other geologic features are permanent and unchanging. In truth, lakes constantly change with wind direction, rainfall, and other factors. Study the map of Escanaba Lake (see fig. 13.1) to determine the lake's source of water. Is there evidence of inflow and outflow? How does this compare with Sucker Lake?

9. Hatching tadpoles can be exciting.

   a. Look in nearby ponds for tadpole eggs. Look for clumpy, gelatinous masses encasing small dark spots. The best time to look for eggs is when the water temperature starts to rise in the spring. This usually occurs in March or April in the northern United States.

b. Collect the tadpole eggs using a small household strainer. Collect about one quarter cup of egg mass. When you collect the eggs, collect about eight gallons (2 buckets) of pond water.

c. Put the eggs and pond water in a 10-gallon aquarium. If the aquarium has no aerator, replace about half of the water every other day. This will entail collecting more water from the pond and bringing it to the classroom.

d. When the tadpoles begin to hatch, sprinkle commercial fish food on the water.

e. Make a journal containing sketches and written descriptions of the hatching and growth of the tadpoles. Keep about 7–10 of the tadpoles and return the rest to the pond. When the tadpoles you have kept begin to grow legs, return them to the pond, too.

10. For settlers a source of fresh water was a prime consideration in deciding where to settle. Water is needed for drinking, transportation, cleaning, cooking, and other vital uses. Locate the major metropolitan areas of your state to learn their proximity to oceans, rivers, lakes, canals, or other bodies of water. In the library media center research the role of water in the settlement of your state. What is the water source for your area? How did it contribute to the founding and growth of the town? Does it still contribute in terms of economics or recreation? Has flood or drought affected the area?

11. Keep a turtle in the classroom.

a. Place a 3-inch layer of sand on the bottom of a 10-gallon aquarium. Add several rocks and about 3 gallons of water. Be sure that some of the rocks protrude above the water line.

b. Put the aquarium in a sunny spot so the turtle can sun itself. Feed it commercial turtle food.

c. Every two or three days, dip out about one-third of the water and replace it with fresh water.

d. For more information about the care and feeding of turtles, read books in the library media center. Look for *Turtles: A Complete Pet Owners Manual to Understanding and Caring for Turtles*, by Hartmut Wilkie (Hauppage, NY: Barrons Educational Service, 1983). Note: Turtles can spread salmonella. Students must wear rubber gloves if the turtle is to be handled. It is also important to keep the turtle's container clean.

12. One of Wil's greatest pleasures was to carefully observe animals and then write descriptions of them or draw them. Observe a classroom or family pet and write a description of its behavior. Pantomime some of its movements.

13. Wil was alone on his island but he never felt lonely. Write about a time when you were happy to be alone. Describe the setting or tell when it happened, but do not feel obliged to reveal personal information that you prefer to keep private. With the class discuss why people sometimes need to be alone and how it feels.

14. Wil spent many hours thinking about his grandmother before he could write about her. There are many things we do not know about our grandparents or our parents, for example, their school days, early jobs, how they met, or stories they heard from their parents and grandparents. Talk to older members of your family about their early lives. Some may have come from other states or countries; some may have served in wars or participated in other historic events. Interview an older person to find out how his or her life and the

world have changed in the past few decades. Ask to see old photographs to add another dimension to the conversation. Pick one person to write about as Wil wrote about his grandmother.

15. Interview people who have been active or are well known in your community. Or, research events that had great impact on the community. Write about these people or events and compile the reports to create a local history of your community.

16. Most people have much less experience than Wil had swimming in freshwater ponds or lakes. Discuss the differences between swimming holes and swimming pools. Talk to parents or grandparents about where they swam as children and where they prefer to swim now.

17. The shell of a turtle is an example of geometric symmetry. Design a species of turtle to add to the 180 freshwater species already identified by scientists. Be sure to name the new species. To learn more about turtles read "Freshwater Turtles—Design for Survival" Christopher P. White in *National Geographic* (volume 169, no. 1, January 1986).

Fig. 13.2. Turtle Shell.

18. Gary Paulsen, author of *The Island,* writes about places he has lived and events in his life. Read "Gary Paulsen: Artist–with–Words," in *Teaching Pre–K–8,* (August–September 1992).

19. Many lakes and coastal areas are being developed as recreational areas. Space to build vacation homes or to park campers and other recreational vehicles is in great demand. This development can put stress on the environment. Role play a situation involving the development of Sucker Lake. Coastal Realty wants to develop land on all sides of the lake. A small area would be set aside as public property for boat launching, swimming, and picnicking. All other areas, except for some private parcels of land, would be divided into one-acre lots, which would be sold for $10,000–$18,000. The main characters in this scenario are:

- Richard White, owner of Coastal Realty, which gets an 8-percent commission of lot sales.

- Bernard and Valerie Shearing, who own about 75 percent of the land around the lake. The land has been in the family for many generations, but the Shearings live in Madison, Wisconsin. There are rumors that Mr. Shearing is heavily in debt.

- Stephen Gillis, who owns hundreds of acres of land next to the area that Coastal Realty wants to develop. If the Coastal Realty deal succeeds, it will be easy for Gillis to develop his land, too.

- Department of Environmental Protection officials, who feel the lake is too small to withstand development.

- Audubon Society members, who agree with the Department of Environmental Protection. The Audubon Society is especially concerned about the lake's resident bird population and the use of the area by migrating birds.

- Tom McFarland, a biologist at the state university who knows that the species of turtle Wil observed is very close to becoming endangered.

- Public Utilities Commission officials, who believe it is economically unsound to provide sewage service and other necessary services to the lake area.

- the Maypine Tourist Bureau, which has been promoting this area of Wisconsin as a vacation area. The tourist bureau welcomes developments or other attractions that will entice people to the area.

- Chad and Amanda Clark, year-round residents of a cabin on the lake. They feel their way of life is threatened by the encroachment of vacationers. The cabin is the Clark's only property, and Mr. Clark does seasonal work in the logging industry.

- the Pinewood Council of Boy Scouts, Methodist Youth Fellowship, and Young Ones Day Care Center, all of which use the beach and surrounding areas for day trips and overnight camping.

- other citizens who have an interest in the lake, for or against development.

Role play discussions among the various people and interest groups. Then role play a Maypine Zoning Commission hearing at which individuals and representatives of each interest group state their cases. Based on the arguments presented, the zoning commission will decide whether or not to allow development around the lake.

Resources

Topographical maps are excellent tools for studying landforms. The maps are sold at sporting goods stores, bookstores, or some government agencies. To locate a specific map, you need a map index and catalog for the state in which the area is located. You can obtain catalogs, indexes, and maps from USGS Map Sales, Box 25286, Denver, CO 80225. The name of the topographical map for the Escanaba Lake area is White Sand Lake quadrangle map (number N4600-W8930/7.5).

If you have little experience with topographical maps, order a teacher information packet or a folder entitled "Topographical Map Symbols" from USGS Earth Science Information Center, 507 National Center, Reston, VA 22092.

Another source of topographical maps is Map Express in Denver, (303) 987-9384. You may order by phone with a credit card.

An excellent resource on pond life is *Pond Life: A Guide to Common Plants and Animals of North American Ponds and Lakes,* by George K. Reid and Herbert Zim (New York: Golden Press, 1967).

Related Titles

"Gary Paulsen: Artist-with-Words." *Teaching Pre-K-8* 23, no. 1 (August-September 1992): 52.

Reid, George K., and Herbert Zim. *Pond Life: A Guide to Common Plants and Animals of North American Ponds and Lakes*. New York: Golden Press, 1967.

White, Christopher P. "Freshwater Turtles—Design for Survival." *National Geographic* 169, no. 1 (January 1986): 40-59.

Wilkie, Hartmut. *Turtles: A Complete Pet Owners Manual to Understanding and Caring for Turtles*. Hauppage, NY: Barrons Educational Service, 1983.

Chapter 14
Wetlands

The Talking Earth
Jean Craighead George
New York: Harper & Row, 1983

Summary

Billie Wind cannot resolve the conflict between her modern American lifestyle and Seminole traditions until she has ventured into the Everglades long enough to hear the animals talk. Befriended by an otter named Petang and a panther called Coootchobee, she canoes through the swampy, sloughy land called the River of Grass. Even in this wilderness area she sees signs of encroaching civilization as she searches for her spirit.

Earth Concepts

Everglades, River of Grass; swamps; soil and rocks; movement of water above and below ground; weather and weather forecasting; temperature; humidity; storms; vegetation; salinity

Environmental Concepts

Relation of plant and animal life, dependence of animal species on fresh water, forest fires, effect of people and natural forces on the earth, environmental awareness, nature versus society in the struggle to control the environment, urban growth, short-term versus long-term effects of changes in nature

General Concepts

Cultural diversity and awareness, Seminole culture and customs, Seminole culture versus modern culture, rites of passage from adolescence to adulthood, attitudinal changes about life and nature

Activities

1. Before you start to read *The Talking Earth,* learn about the weather in Florida. Read newspapers or listen to television weather forecasts. Check the temperature, humidity, precipitation, and storm patterns. If you have friends or relatives in Florida, ask for permission to call them to ask about the weather. Because all of Florida does not experience the same weather, you may study just one region, a major metropolitan area, or the area described in *The Talking Earth.*

2. Study a map of southern Florida to find the area in which the story is set. Locate the Gulf of Mexico, Everglades National Park, Big Cypress National Preserve, and Big Cypress Seminole Indian Reservation. Using the map's key or legend, make inferences about this area of the state, for example, landforms, population density, and modes of transportation.

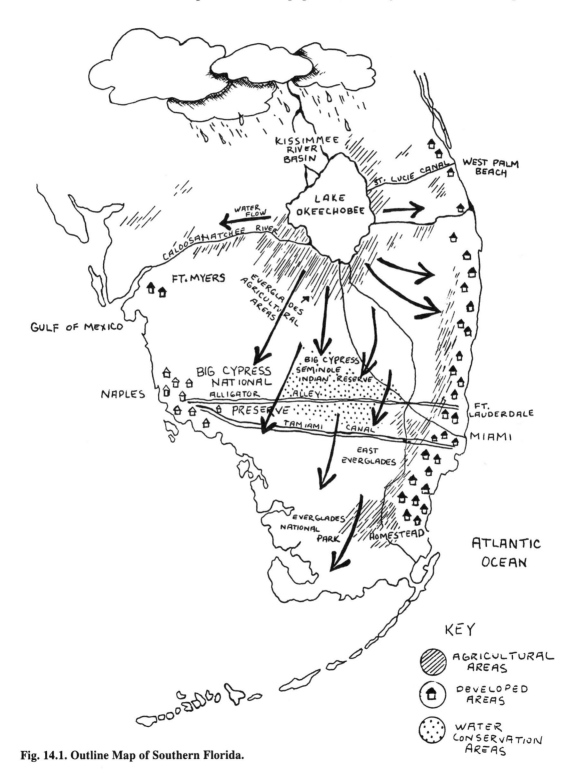

Fig. 14.1. Outline Map of Southern Florida.

3. Figure 14.2A is a schematic drawing of southern Florida, showing cities, canals, agricultural lands, highways, and Everglades National Park. Figure 14.2B is a schematic map of this area about 100 years ago.

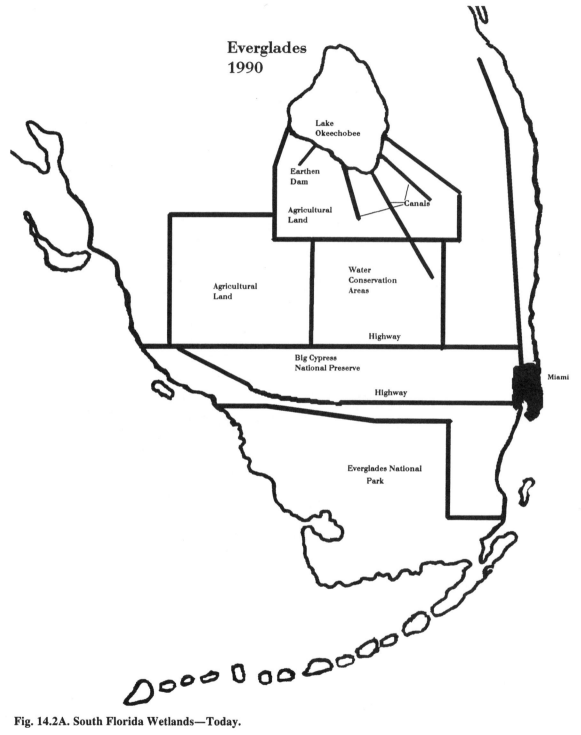

Everglades 1990

Lake Okeechobee

Earthen Dam

Agricultural Land

Canals

Agricultural Land

Water Conservation Areas

Highway

Big Cypress National Preserve

Highway

Miami

Everglades National Park

Fig. 14.2A. South Florida Wetlands—Today.

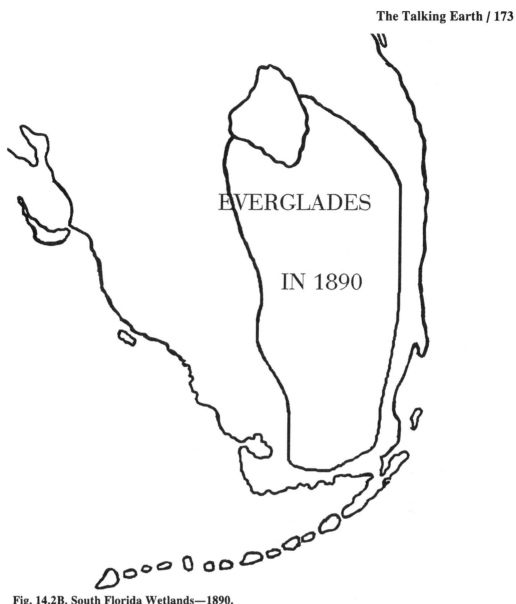

Fig. 14.2B. South Florida Wetlands—1890.

a. Study the two maps to compare the size of the Everglades. What impediments to the natural flow of water have been built during the past 100 years? What effect have they had on the size of the Everglades?

b. To see the effect of the impediments on the land, assume there is a heavy rainfall in the Lake Okeechobee region. On each map draw arrows to indicate the movement of the runoff from the higher ground of Lake Okeechobee to the lower areas to the south. What do you learn by comparing the drainage systems on the two maps?

4. Before you begin to read the book, list words you associate with Florida, for example, Disney World, oranges, beaches, retirement homes, or hurricanes. As you read the book add words to the list. After you read the book note how the list has changed. Using the words in your final list, make a travel poster to advertise the state and its many attractions (see fig. 14.3, p. 174). You may even wish to let your words form the outline of the state.

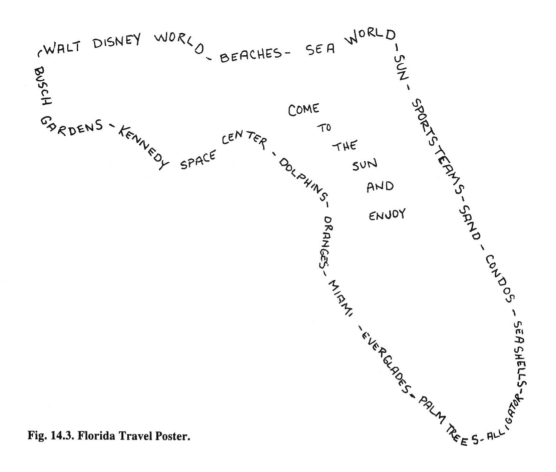

Fig. 14.3. Florida Travel Poster.

5. Most of the water in the Everglades flows over bedrock of porous limestone. To demonstrate how well limestone holds water, use white ornamental limestone from a garden supply store.

   a. Weigh the bag of dry rock.

   b. Place the rocks in a large bucket of water for 20–30 minutes. Observe the changes.

   c. Remove the limestone and weigh it again. Calculate the difference between the weights after and before soaking the rock. Express the increase as a percentage of the original weight.

   d. Repeat the activity with various types of rock. To compare the sponge-like qualities of the limestone and other rocks, compare the percentage increase in weight after soaking.

   This activity illustrates that the Everglades is a gigantic, porous sponge. If the water is removed from this area, the Everglades would cease to exist and the land would cave in.

6. Jar ponds show the interrelationship of plants and animals. Each jar is a closed ecosystem. The jar ponds could last all year.

   a. Work in small groups. Obtain a large, glass or clear plastic container with a lid. Provide students with 2–3 gallon jars with lids. (The school careteria may be able to supply these.)

b. Place a small amount of sand in the bottom of the jar.

c. Fill the jar almost full with pond water or tap water. If you use tap water, allow it to rest for 48 hours before adding living organisms. It is better to use pond water, if possible.

d. Add rooted aquatic plants like *Elodea* and floating aquatic plants like duckweed. These can be gathered from freshwater ponds or purchased at an aquarium store.

e. Add small animals like snails, small fish, and water insects. These can be gathered from freshwater ponds or purchased at an aquarium store.

f. Seal the jar and place it in a sunny window. Allow two or three days for the ecosystem to develop. Be careful that the jar does not become warmer than room temperature.

g. Observe the jar carefully over a period of several days or weeks. Keep a journal of your thoughts, observations, and answers to questions, for example

> How does the closed ecosystem differ from natural ecosystems?
>
> What food chains exist in the jar pond?
>
> What is the ecological niche or role of each organism, plant, and animal?
>
> What roles are performed by organisms you cannot see with the naked eye? Use a microscope or hand lens to observe them.

Fig. 14.4. Plastic Jar Ponds.

> What are the shapes and forms of the microscopic animals?
>
> What happens to the energy from the sun as it shines on the jar pond?
>
> Periodically make a population count of each type of plant and animal in your ecosystem. How do they change? Use bar graphs to show the changes.

7. Soil study is necessary to understanding the Everglades. See activities two through five in chapter 1.

8. An interesting way to learn about a topic is to write a book to share with younger children. Write the ABCs of the Everglades, for example, *A* is for alligator, *B* is for bromeliads, *C* is for cypress, and so forth. Illustrate the book and bind it in a folder or other binder. Ask the library media specialist to include your book in the library media center collection.

   When writing an ABC book, certain rules should be followed.

   - Focus on one topic. For example, if your book is about birds, don't include mammals. Be creative with the words you use for *X, Y,* and *Z,* but stay true to the topic of the book.

   - Use one part of speech—verbs, nouns, or adjectives— throughout.

   - Use words that begin with the sound of the first letter. Do not use words that begin with a silent *k* or with *ph.*

   - Single words are usually used in ABC books, but entire sentences containing the word in boldface are more and more common. For example, you might write "*A* is for alligator" or you might write "The American alligator is endangered."

   - Be sure the illustrations are obviously related to the topic.

   - Select an age level for your audience. Use words that are familiar or not too difficult for children that age.

9. The U.S. Fish and Wildlife Service lists species of animals that are endangered in North America. Five of these species can be found in Florida: the American alligator, the American crocodile, the Atlantic salt marsh snake, the Florida panther, and the southeastern beach mouse. Using information from *The Talking Earth* and your own knowledge, make some inferences about why these animals are becoming endangered. Research a particular animal or the plight of wild animals in general to determine the causes of depleted animal populations. How does animal depletion affect the ecosystem? Are any measures being taken to protect wildlife? What will happen if no effort is made to protect these animals? Do we need to worry if certain species become extinct? Why?

10. List the animals and plants mentioned as Billie makes her trip through the Everglades. Classify the animals as mammals, birds, insects, amphibians, reptiles, fish, or mollusks. Classify the plants as algae, fungi, mosses, ferns, and flowering plants. Be sure you have a reason for classifying the plants and animals as you do. Use books from the library media center to help you.

11. Fill in the blanks in the following puzzle with the names of plants and animals found in the Everglades. Clues following the puzzle will help you fill in the blanks.

    a.   _ _ _ _ E _ _ _ _

    b.   _ V _ _ _ _ _

    c.   _ E _ _ _ _

    d.   _ R _ _ _ _ _

    e.   _ _ _ G _ _ _ _

    f.   _ _ L _

    g.   _ _ A _ _ _

    h.   _ _ _ D _ _ _ _ _ _ _ _

    i.   _ _ _ _ _ E _ _

    j.   _ _ _ S _ _

- Poisonous and nonpoisonous species of this limbless reptile live in swamps.
- This bulbous perennial bears the name of an eight-legged arthropod.
- This tree or shrub lives at the point where fresh water meets salt water.
- These aquatic mammals live in river and coastal waters of Florida but have been hunted to near extinction.
- Often purple, these flowers are considered rare but grow profusely in the swamps.
- Some varieties of this tall tree produce dates and coconuts.
- The fronds of this low-growing fan palm are used for weaving.
- These wading birds have a distinctive curved bill. They are related to the heron.
- This pear-shaped fruit has green edible pulp.
- Often blue, this aquatic bird has a long, curved neck. (Note: Answers to the puzzle are in the back of the book.)

12. Billie must survive a hurricane. For activities about hurricanes, see activities nine, ten, and eleven in chapter 8.

13. Fresh water is essential to sustain life. It is estimated that each American uses about 75 gallons of water per day.

    a. To help you understand how much water the average American uses in a day, collect and display 75 1-gallon milk jugs.

    b. Use 75 gallons per day to create math problems that show how much fresh water is used in the United States. How much water would all of the students in the classroom use in a day? A week? A month? A year? How much water would be used by all of the students in the school? How much would each family use? Create more questions, and show the answers in a graph.

14. The value of clean water is one of the themes of *The Talking Earth*. Information about this topic is published in *Clean Water Action News*. To find out more about clean water, write to Clean Water Action, 1320 18th Street NW, Third Floor, Washington, DC 20036. To get the address or telephone number of the group's state or regional office, call (202) 457-1286.

15. Preserving wetlands helps to ensure the availability of clean water. If you feel strongly about this issue, write to your Congressional representatives. The library media specialist can help you find the names and addresses of your area's representatives and senators.

16. Droughts sometimes plague Florida. How does a prolonged lack of water affect the quality of life for humans, animals, and vegetation? How does it affect recreation? In prolonged droughts, water use must be restricted. How would you encourage people to conserve water? What would you ask them to give up? If water supplies shrink too much, mandatory restrictions must be enforced. What would you require people to give up? How would you enforce the restrictions? What would the penalties be? To help you with this activity, brainstorm the ways you or your family uses water. List the ways in order of importance. Also brainstorm and rank community needs, such as industry, schools, hospitals, nursing homes, and so forth.

17. Florida is one of the fastest-growing states in the United States. As more and more people move there, previously unused land is being developed for homes and shopping areas. This development produces problems. For example, there is less land for animal habitats, and water supplies will be exhausted. Discuss these problems and their potential for altering the quality of life in Florida.

18. The Everglades provides animal habitats and fresh water for much of southern Florida, including the city of Miami and its suburbs. If the Everglades continues to be drained and developed, the amount of fresh water available to the Miami area will be severely limited. Imagine life in the future if huge portions of the Everglades were drained for development. The supply of fresh water is severely limited and life has changed drastically. Write a story about life in southern Florida under these conditions. Refer to some favorite children's books in which the quality of life was threatened, such as *The Little House,* by Virginia Lee Burton (Boston: Houghton Mifflin, 1969) *The Wump World,* by Bill Peet (New York: Random House, 1971) and *The Lorax,* by Dr. Seuss (Boston: Houghton Mifflin, 1970).

19. Write a story about Billie's adventures from the viewpoint of Petang, the baby otter she rescued. Or, write a story with Petang as the main character.

20. Write acrostics to describe the many animals or plants found in the Everglades. Write the name of the plant or animal as a column so that each letter in the word is on a subsequent line. Use each letter of the animal or plant name as the first letter of an adjective or phrase that describes the animal or plant. For example,

    P rowling

    A nimated

    N octurnal

    T hreatening

    H ungry

    E lusive

    R estless

21. Billie was adept at providing for herself during her journey. One thing she did was weave mats from cattail reeds. If you can obtain cattails or another kind of reed, weave a small mat. Make designs in the mat by using weaving reeds of various shades or by using other forms of vegetation, such as long grasses. Remember that the vegetation will shrink as it dries, so make your weaving tight and sturdy. If you cannot obtain reeds, weave ½-inch strips of paper. When you finish the mat, turn it over, fold the edges of the reeds or paper to the back, and tape them in place.

22. Have a Fruits from Florida healthy snack day. Bring in oranges, grapefruit, tangerines, peaches, nectarines, tangelos, avocados, figs, coconuts, strawberries, and cantaloupes and other melons. Buy foods that are in season, and survey grocery advertisements to get the best buys.

23. To learn about life in rural Florida at other times in history, read *Strawberry Girl,* by Lois Lenski (New York: Dell, 1945), a Newbery award book, or *The Yearling,* by Marjorie Rawlings (New York: Macmillan, 1966). Compare and contrast the lives of the main characters of each of these books and *The Talking Earth.*

24. Watch a video program about the Everglades. As you watch the video

    a. record the names of the plants and animals,

    b. indicate the water resources,

    c. discuss the relationship of the water and the land, and

    d. make inferences about the value of the Everglades.

    One good program is "The Wasting of a Wetland," a documentary by Daniel Elias (1991). The video is available from Bullfrog Films, P.O. Box 149, Oley, PA 18947.

Resources

Several resources can be ordered from the Florida National Parks and Monuments Association, P.O. Box 279, Homestead, FL 33030; (305) 247-1216. These resources include:

Everglades Wildguide, by Jean Craighead George (Washington, D.C.: U.S. Department of the Interior, 1988).

Everglades: The Park Story, by William B. Robertson (Homestead, Fla.: Florida National Parks and Monuments Association, 1988).

Other excellent articles on the resources of Florida and the dangers that threaten them are:

"Man and Manatee," by Fred Bavendam, in *National Geographic* 166, no. 3 (September 1984).

"South Florida Water," by Nicole Duplaix, in *National Geographic* 178, no. 1 (July 1990).

"The Tree Nobody Liked," by Rick Gore, in *National Geographic* 151, no. 5 (May 1977).

A video and software program about the dangers of hurricanes and how the storms are tracked can be ordered from the Weather Channel, (800) 258-2700.

A special edition of *National Geographic* (November 1993) was devoted to fresh water in North America. Topics covered include supply, development, pollution, and restoration of water resources.

Related Titles

Bavendam, Fred. "Man and Manatee." *National Geographic* 166, no. 3 (September 1984): 400-414.

Burton, Virginia Lee. *The Little House*. Boston, MA: Houghton Mifflin, 1969.

Clean Water Action. *Clean Water Action News*. 1320 18th Street NW, Washington, DC 20036.

Duplaix, Nicole. "South Florida Water." *National Geographic* 178, no. 1 (July 1990): 89-113

Elias, Daniel. "The Wasting of a Wetland." (VHS) Oley, PA: Bullfrog Films, 1991.

Geisel, Theodor (Dr. Seuss). *The Lorax*. Boston, MA: Hougton Mifflin, 1970.

George, Jean Craighead. *Everglades Wildguide*. Washington, DC: U.S. Department of the Interior, 1988.

Gore, Rick. "The Tree Nobody Liked." *National Geographic* 151, no. 5 (May 1977): 668-689.

Lenski, Lois. *Strawberry Girl.* New York: Dell, 1945.

Peet, Bill. *The Wump World.* New York: Random House, 1971.

Rawlings, Marjorie. *The Yearling.* New York: Macmillan, 1966.

Robertson, William B. *Everglades: The Park Story.* Homestead, FL: Florida National Parks and Monuments Assn., 1988.

Appendix

Answers to Chapter Questions

Chapter 1, *Sarah, Plain and Tall*

basil	rosemary
dillweed	mint
sage	tarragon
thyme	oregano
marjoram	bay leaf

Chapter 4, *Julie of the Wolves*

lemming	snowy owl
weasel	puffin
musk oxen	caribou
elk	white whale
deer	eider duck
bear	rabbit
ptarmigan	wolverine
walrus	dog

Puzzle solution: Long Arctic Winter

Chapter 5, *The Incredible Journey*

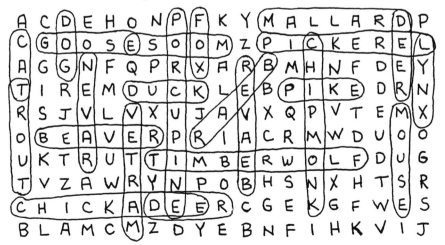

Chapter 6, *Lion Hound*

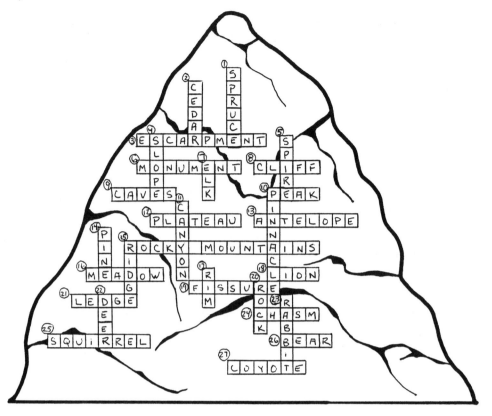

Chapter 14, *The Talking Earth*

palmettos

avocado

herons

orchids

mangrove

palm

snakes

spider plants

manatees

ibises

Index

About the Authors

The Butzows live in Indiana, Pennsylvania, a small University town located in rural western Pennsylvania. They and their two daughters enjoy traveling and have visited all the environments described in this volume including Lyme Regis, England. One room of their home houses an extensive collection of children's and adolescent literature that provides the basis for the research involved in selecting books and developing instructional ideas included in their two books on the use of literature in elementary and middle school instruction

Carol and John both have undergraduate degrees from St. Bonaventure University in New York State. In addition Carol completed master's degrees in history from Colgate University and in reading education from the University of Maine. Carol's doctoral degree in elementary education was earned at Indiana University of Pennsylvania. John's master's degree was earned at St. Bonaventure and his doctorate in science education came from the University of Rochester. Carol has many years of experience teaching at the middle-junior high level as well as at the college level. John originally worked as a teacher of science and university science educator and more recently has been a university administrator.

John and Carol have traveled extensively throughout the United States including Alaska to present workshops, inservice courses, and conferences. They have also spoken to audiences in Canada, Scotland, and Sweden. For information on workshops or conference presentations please contact them through Libraries Unlimited.

From **Teacher Ideas Press**

U.S. HISTORY THROUGH CHILDREN'S LITERATURE
From the Colonial Period to World War II
Wanda J. Miller

Enhance the study of U.S. history with historical fiction and nonfiction. Stepping back in time to experience a character's dilemmas, thoughts, feelings, and actions helps students more easily grasp and retain a true understanding of an era. Here is all the material you need to begin a literature-based history program. **Grades 4–8**.
xiv, 229p. 8½x11 paper ISBN 1-56308-440-6

WRITING THROUGH CHILDREN'S AND YOUNG ADULT LITERATURE, GRADES 4–8
From Authors to Authorship
Mary Strong and Mimi Neamen

This acclaimed book uses students' natural responses to literature to guide them into creative action. It teaches the writing process naturally, using published works as the basis for writing experiences. Literature-based writing ideas, examples of students' writing, and vignettes that describe students at work on different projects are included. **Grades 4–8**.
xi, 173p. 8½x11 paper ISBN 1-56308-038-9

CHANCES ARE
Hands-on Activities in Probability and Statistics, Grades 3-7
Shela Dolgowich, Helen M. Lounsbury, and Barry G. Muldoon

Fun with statistics? Chances are *yes* with this resource! Through simple and enjoyable learning experiences, this hands-on activity book explains a variety of mathematical concepts that are directly tied to the NCTM Standards. A comprehensive, easy-to-use teacher guide; reproducible activity sheets; and manipulatives accompany each activity. **Grades 3–7**. *(Great for the multiage classroom.)*
xviii, 125p. 8½x11 paper ISBN 1-56308-314-0

THE INVENTIVE MIND IN SCIENCE
Creative Thinking Activities
Christine Ebert and Edward S. Ebert II

Creativity is not just a gift of a select few—it can be tapped in all. Delve into an in-depth discussion of creative thinking and its role in science. More than 50 exciting,mind-stretching activities integrate the processesof creativity and invention into the science curriculum. **Grades 4–8**.
xii, 109p. 8½x11 paper ISBN 1-56308-387-6

THE BEANSTALK AND BEYOND
Developing Critical Thinking Through Fair Tales
Joan M. Wolf

Turn fairy tales and fairy-tale characters into a springboard for learning with this enchanting book! A multitude of activities challenge students to move beyond the simplistic study of fairy tales to develop problem-solving, critical-thinking, and creative-writing skills. **Grades 4–8**.
xiii, 133p. 8½x11 paper ISBN 1-56308-482-1

For a FREE catalog or to place an order, please contact:

Teacher Ideas Press
Dept. B86 · P.O. Box 6633 · Englewood, CO 80155-6633
1-800-237-6124, ext. 1 · Fax: 303-220-8843 · E-mail: lu-books@lu.com

Check out our Web site!
www.lu.com/tip